# Realizing Our Divinity

## THE CHANGE WE NEED

## CURTIS A VIGNESS

**BALBOA.**
PRESS

A DIVISION OF HAY HOUSE

Balboa Press books may be ordered through booksellers or by contacting:

Balboa Press
A Division of Hay House
1663 Liberty Drive
Bloomington, IN 47403
www.balboapress.com
1 (877) 407-4847

Because of the dynamic nature of the Internet, any web addresses or
links contained in this book may have changed since publication and
may no longer be valid. The views expressed in this work are solely those
of the author and do not necessarily reflect the views of the publisher,
and the publisher hereby disclaims any responsibility for them.

The author of this book does not dispense medical advice or prescribe the use
of any technique as a form of treatment for physical, emotional, or medical
problems without the advice of a physician, either directly or indirectly. The
intent of the author is only to offer information of a general nature to help
you in your quest for emotional and spiritual well-being. In the event you use
any of the information in this book for yourself, which is your constitutional
right, the author and the publisher assume no responsibility for your actions.

Any people depicted in stock imagery provided by Thinkstock are models,
and such images are being used for illustrative purposes only.
Certain stock imagery © Thinkstock.

Printed in the United States of America.

ISBN: 978-1-4525-8331-0 (sc)
ISBN: 978-1-4525-8333-4 (hc)
ISBN: 978-1-4525-8332-7 (e)

Library of Congress Control Number: 2013917836

Balboa Press rev. date: 11/15/2013

*If you want to see change in the world,*
*you have to be the change.*

—Mahatma Gandhi

This book is dedicated to all who aspire to create a better life for themselves and all living beings.

# Contents

# Part 2: The Human Experience

# Part 3: The Path

## *Part 4: Moving Forward*

# Introduction

I was raised to believe certain things about life that didn't always make sense to me. What I believed to be the truth of my existence always left lingering questions burning inside of me. It wasn't until I started to question those fundamental beliefs that I was able to see beyond the limits of my mind. I was able to see a connection we all share but very few people notice today. A connection far greater than anything I was taught or could have believed possible.

This book is a brief overview of a wide range of topics as they relate to our inner divinity and our connections to each other and all living beings. My goal is not to press my personal beliefs upon anyone else. My intentions are to get people to notice the vastness of our existence and question the world we have inherited. I want people to understand that life does not have to be a challenge, and love can replace fear and hatred. For far too long, we have disassociated from our divine consciousness and have been driven by an unconscious mind into the world of separateness, greed, and hatred; this is what causes so much suffering today. We have lost sight of who we truly are.

As you read the words of this book, one of three things may happen: something will come alive inside you, you may disagree, or you will be completely indifferent to what I have written, because not everyone is at the point of wanting to know the truth about our existence. I recommend you read it from the beginning. It may be tempting to start out at certain places and skip from one topic to another, but I have laid out the book in such a way as to explain things in a specific order. What you may read in one chapter may not make sense until you have read the foundation provided in a previous section. Don't use your mind to try and understand what I am saying. Rather, allow the words to sink in. The mind will try to reject the true meaning, but if you allow the words to resonate an understanding will emerge. As the layers of the ego are pealed back the words here will begin to make more sense.

This is not a quick fix or "paint-by-numbers" self-help book. There is no magic potion, and you will not find your life's answers here, because what you are seeking can only be found within yourself. All I can do is point you in a direction. Hopefully, some of the things I have written here may open your eyes to something you may not have considered before.

Each topic could easily be a book in and of itself. But what I am trying to do is share a general idea about portions of what we each believe to be the truth about life, and possibly expose you to a new way of looking at the world. I want to encourage you to examine what you believe to be real and make you question the things about your current beliefs that don't make sense.

Throughout the course of this book I will use words like "God," "Space," "Source," "Energy," and "Infinity." These words are used to express an understanding of a supreme Being or a divine consciousness. I use such words because they are limitless in their meaning and use, and because their lack of limitation is incomprehensible to our human understanding, which is why most spiritual teachers and scientists use words like these to describe something that cannot be explained in words. The God most of us have been raised to believe in is far more vast and indescribable than we have made Him out to be by constricting His existence to our limited intelligence and our even more limited vocabulary.

This book is intended for anyone who wishes to make a better life for himself or herself and wants to do his or her part in our future advancement as a species. I begin by explaining our truest existence. In part 1, I explain why it is important we realize our divinity. I describe the space that is Infinity, which we are all a part of. I give a brief history of our species and explain how we have evolved throughout history. I note some of the errors made in the way we have been taught to think and continue to think. And I finish this part by describing our purpose for existing in the first place.

In part 2, I explain how our relationships with each other have caused us to create the fear and hatred we experience today. I go into detail on how we can better our relationships to create a more peaceful existence.

Part 3 is slightly different from the rest of the book. Here I use the analogy of a path to describe our life, both in physical form and beyond. I discuss the path of life before we entered this world, our time here on this planet, and the time after we leave our bodies.

Part 4 is the conclusion. I provide insight into the shape of the current state of our world. I explain the importance of discovering our innermost divinity to save ourselves and all other living things from self-destruction.

My hope is that by reading this book, you may realize the mistakes in thinking humanity has made throughout the past. I want you to see the promise of a future where we all realize our connection to each other.

Over the past several years, I have made some drastic changes to the way I look at life. I have begun to see things in a much broader sense. I began a spiritual practice that makes my religious upbringing pale in comparison. I have a much clearer understanding of whom I truly am and where I come from than was ever taught to me in church or in any formal education class.

Surely, most people have some idea or set of beliefs about the unknown. Those in the religious world have their beliefs, scientist theirs, and some people simply don't care. Then there are people like me, who want to have a better understanding of it all. In learning the answers to the questions I had about life and trying to find what I thought was missing, I finally realized there was nothing missing at all. What I used to feel as sort of a void was nothing more than my mind believing in something that simply wasn't real.

In my personal life, I have stopped trying to obtain or become anything. I have gained a sense of simply being in the world. I found the reason I created problems for myself was nothing more than my disconnection from the creator of life, God, and what I grew up believing God to be is completely different from what I now know.

I know fear is the most toxic emotion we harbor as individuals and as a society. A fear that doesn't have its origin in some mystical, evil entity but is, in fact, the creation of our own disillusioned human mind. I learned that when I am connected to the Source of life, I have the power to create for myself the things I want with very little effort. I found stress is nothing more than the resistance of life's natural progression. I have become healthier by knowing my body is a direct reflection of my thoughts, that "We become what we continuously think about," as Ralph Waldo Emerson points out. Also, I have learned a detached relationship is the only healthy and highly functional way a relationship will ever work.

As a result of these insights, I discovered an indescribable feeling of peace. I have a new understanding about life that changed me as a person. I can finally see that every living being is a part of something much bigger than it may appear on the surface. And a knowing we are all one.

All this and much more are what I intend to share with you. I am happy and thankful to be where I am in life, and I want the same for everyone else with whom I share this planet.

Somewhere in the words of this book, may you find that spark within yourself, as well. Then you may begin to understand who you truly are and seek for yourself the answers to the questions you undoubtedly have about yourself and the universe you call home. Every living being deserves to feel peace and stillness in their lives. If you are living with such stillness within yourself, you know what I mean. If you are seeking this peace, you will surely find it, because just having an open mind and questioning things until they make sense are all it takes to begin to attract the answers. If you don't know what you are looking for, perhaps all you need is a little guidance.

It has been an amazing experience for me to write all this down. I have always used writing to express to myself how I feel, but this is the first time I have ever shared it with anyone else. I have learned far more in writing this book than I could ever hope to give anyone reading it. I hope all of you who take the time to read it will find at least a spark within yourself that may one day ignite the inner presence within to come alive and be noticed. The change we need begins when we realize our divinity.

With Love,

Curtis A Vigness

*The coming of the kingdom of heaven cannot be observed, and no one will announce, "Look, here it is," or "There it is." For behold, the kingdom of heaven is among you.*

—Luke 17:20-21

# Part 1

# Understanding Our Existence

# 1

## Why This Is Important

*Mastery of life is not a question of control, but of finding
a balance between human and being.*

-Eckhart Tolle

D o you ever wonder who we truly are and where we came
from? Does the chaos you see in society cause you to
question the ideology and teachings of our ancestors? Do
you ever stop to consider our purpose for existing? What can we do
to create a better life? How can we improve our relationships with
each other? How do we stop the destruction of the planet and live
in peace and harmony with all life forms?

In trying to understand the answers to all these questions, and
hundreds more like them, I have been led on a journey, a journey
to uncover the secret to the greatest mysteries of our existence. I
have always been fascinated with the unknown in this world, in the
universe surrounding us, and in what lies beyond what we cannot
comprehend.

In trying to gain a better understanding of it all, I tried to
learn all I could to help it make sense to me. I contemplated such
questions throughout my youth and into my adult life. I couldn't
understand the way the world operates, the horrible way people
treated each other, and the destructive way we, as a species, have

been destroying our planet. I couldn't figure out why there was such hate in our society. I couldn't understand why such a small portion of the world held the majority of the wealth and allowed the rest of the world to suffer and struggle. I couldn't fathom the idea of people killing each other by the millions throughout history just for a piece of land, in the name of their god, or for the earth's natural resources. *This cannot be our existence,* I thought. *This can't be why God put us here.*

This book is a direct reflection of my view of the world as I have come to understand things. I have always been thoroughly intrigued by life, both here and beyond what scientists and religious leaders know and understand. I was raised to believe a certain set of religious ideals. As I got older, I had lingering questions about life and the world that just could not be answered by religious teachings or science books. Religion taught me I should have faith and believe in the unknown. But I couldn't accept what I was supposed to have faith in. A lot of the things I was taught about science and religion didn't add up to me. And I couldn't shake the persisting questions I tried to understand.

On the surface, my life was fine. But inside, I felt a longing. I couldn't describe it, and yet I knew it could never be satisfied with anything in the physical realm. The world I grew up knowing didn't make much sense to me. With my religious upbringing, I couldn't decipher the contradictory ideas being taught to me. This added to the confusion I felt about life.

At a fairly young age, I began to try to mask the hole I felt inside with external things, worldly things. I used different substances to try to cover up or numb the feelings I had inside. I bounced from one failed relationship to another, looking to find some sort of happiness. I acquired the material things I thought would make me happy. When I got tired of one job, I moved on to another. I moved around the country looking for my place, and each new place always seemed to be a disappointment. I felt a constant pull I didn't understand, because I didn't feel like I was being pulled in any particular direction. I was looking for answers outside myself and finding nothing.

Nearly everyone is experiencing or has experienced this in life. This "hole" inside is nothing more than our inner Being, our consciousness, trying to break through the hard shell the ego, our human mind, has built inside us. We suffer constantly trying to satisfy the ego without even realizing our mind creates all the suffering and desire we live with. It wasn't until I learned to look inward that I was able to see this as truth. I was able to see who I truly am and realized we are all the same. We are all divine beings, interconnected and inseparable from each other and from God. This separation has brought about the current state of the world.

The world, as we have come to know it, is in a period of rapid change. The ideas and beliefs of the past are being replaced by something much greater. A transformation of our consciousness is upon us. There has never been a time like the present for such a change to take place. We can see a separation from our old beliefs, which have restricted our growth for centuries. We are fed up with corruption, greed, and the fulfillment of the violent and murderous agendas of our world leaders, which have dominated us throughout history.

People see chaos taking place and long for something more, perhaps a comfort of sorts, which causes us to question the most fundamental things we believe to be true. We are beginning to question the ideologies and beliefs of our forefathers, and for good reason. We question our old beliefs and look for ways to change for the betterment of all living things. This has brought forth a transformation, which started long ago with people like the Buddha and Jesus Christ. This transformation is a reconnection with the Energy that created us, allowing our consciousness to evolve to the point where it is noticed more today than ever.

Our old belief systems failed to bring a lasting sense of peace to all living things. Throughout history we have watched as millions upon millions of people were senselessly wiped off the planet all for the acquisition of power, for avarice, and for an ideology whose time has passed.

We see it still. Greed and the lust for power continue to dominate the world. But a revolution is under way, a revolution in terms of our consciousness and our connection to the divine. This revolution will bring about the end of suffering as we know it. It will bring a rise in the joy and peace of the entire planet.

Many people don't realize this, because they are too focused on their day-to-day, mind-driven lives to see beyond what we perceive to be real. Many people believe such drastic change is elusive and the world contains too much evil for any single person to make a difference. But it is possible. In fact, it is our divine destiny!

The world is growing weary of the tyranny and oppression that has brought about the madness before us today. We are fighting wars all over the planet, which only account for unnecessary deaths and more suffering. And nothing is accomplished in the furtherance of humankind. Unfortunately, this has been the norm throughout most of humanity's history. But people are finally getting fed up with the senseless violence and bloodshed and are taking action to make changes. People are uniting against elected officials and dictators, demanding equality and fairness, not as a favor, but as a basic human right. We see people stand up to radical rulers—even knowing they may be killed in the process—all in hope of a better life, a life where people are free from tyranny and oppression, where starvation is a word of the past, and where greed and violence are gone from society.

Many people are on a quest for knowledge. In growing numbers, they want to understand whom they truly are and where they came from. People are tired of being told the same stories heard for generations. These stories have done little to bring about a world of peace and love. They have caused death and destruction on an unimaginable scale, and furthered division among our race and among all living things.

You might wonder how long it will take to find the answers to what you are looking for. I promise you everything you want to know is already inside you and has always been there. All I am doing is reminding you, guiding you to something you have always known. All you have to do is look for the truth, and it will reveal itself to you.

There is a reason you seek the truth. Some people seek it because of grief, some through the frustration of having hit rock bottom, and others may do so just because they're curious. Whatever the reason, we are transitioning to a better, more peaceful world, a world where love replaces all fears. It may be hard to see now, but rest assured it is happening. There are people who live a life where *real* love prevails and whose minds do not control their every action. These people are very few in number now, but the numbers are growing.

Most people would have never reached this state of truth-seeking in the past without some traumatic event, or constant teaching and training from an enlightened master to bring them into an awakened state of being. But we have evolved to the point where people are gravitating toward this truth based on the evolution of our global consciousness. We no longer have to suffer through the pain to be pushed into our self-discovery of who we really are and where we come from.

When you have suffered long enough from the constant chatter of the voices in your head, and you have listened to enough advice from other people just as lost as you, there is nowhere else to look but within. The moment you decide to look inside yourself, your life will never be the same again. I cannot tell you how this transformation of thought will change you individually, but I can say you will experience life much more fully when you realize the connection we share with all of life.

I may challenge your current beliefs, and I hope to provide ideas for creating happiness and abundance in your life. If you don't currently have any real or solid beliefs about where we come from and where we will go when we leave this life, these words will hopefully inspire you to examine these topics further and get you to question what you have been taught. My intentions are not to sell you an idea or a concept. I am not trying to turn you away from anything you believe. I am simply providing a new perspective.

Your life will never change or get better or easier until you figure out your own path. I encourage you to look on the world with an open mind. Don't take anything at face value, and question everything until you are satisfied with the answers. My hope is this book will leave you wanting to know more. Forget what you've been taught. If the old ways worked, you wouldn't be seeking answers. Keep in mind no one, regardless of his or her greatness, can give you all the answers to all life's questions. He or she can only point you in the direction of what you already know. We each have to find our own way. We each have a path, a purpose unique to us. We are all the distinct, individual descendants of a perfect and infinite God, yet we are all one. Just knowing that much, we can begin to realize our divinity.

# 2

## _Space_

_All that can be seen, all that can be imagined, all that remains to be discovered is created from the ever-present energy of Space._

A young boy looked up at his father as the two sat quietly gazing into the night sky. The boy asked, "Father, how far does the sky go?"

The father looked down at the boy and explained, "The sky goes on forever. All that's out there is space; it never ends."

With an interested look, the boy asked, "Well, if there is only space up there, where does God live?"

The father, surprised at the little boy's inquiry, answered, "God lives everywhere."

The boy, now even more confused, asked, "Why can't we see him then?"

"God is everywhere. Everything you can see is God. Every living thing, and even everything that isn't alive. The stars in the sky, and even all the space between everything you see is all God. But God isn't something you can see with your eyes. God is the energy within the space that makes up everything, because without all that energy, and all that space, nothing could exist."

"Why?"

"Because space makes everything what it is. Without space, everything would just blend together. You wouldn't be able to tell the difference between yourself and a chair, or even between the stars and planets if there was no space to separate it all. The space is what separates us and makes us all different. But it is also the one thing that holds us all together."

"So without God, we wouldn't exist?"

"That's right. But without us, God wouldn't exist, either."

Now the boy was really puzzled. He looked at his father and asked, "Why wouldn't God exist without us?"

With a half-smile his father explained, "God is the energy of space, and space goes on forever. Space doesn't start, and it never stops. Without us God wouldn't need a name, because he would be all there is. God is always around us, because he is the space we live in. God is the energy that gives everything life. He makes the grass grow, our hearts beat, and our lungs breath."

The boy, trying to absorb all he had learned, returned his gaze toward the sky and smiled.


The significance of this story is to illustrate that few of us know more than a small child when it comes to the enormity of our existence. We have all, at some point in our lives, looked out at the night sky and wondered what lies beyond or considered how far space can stretch.

Even with the greatest advances in modern technology, scientists are still perplexed at the vastness of space. There are no answers to the questions of where space begins and where it ends. Even if there were an answer, what would lie on the other side of that seemingly endless space?

Scientists believe that even before the big bang occurred, there had to be something; the entire makeup of the universe did not just form out of nothing. If we examine the idea of a big bang, something had to explode or crash into something else to cause such a commotion. But where did such objects come from? Scientists theorize that before there were particles in space large enough to be noticed, a sort of dust lingered throughout space. And as the dust started to cling together, it began to form larger and larger objects. These objects just soared around throughout space, until one day they just happened to collide, causing the "bang." But what created the dust to begin with? We could ponder that subject for eternity.

This "dust," as it were, contained all the elements that make up the universe and our world today. These elements make up all nonliving and living things alike, even us. So the big bang was a cataclysmic event that set into motion the origin of what we know today as our universe, including our own planet. But everything we can see, touch, taste, and smell is made up of the same material that originally formed the universe! What we experience as our physical reality is a combination of all the elements of space, hydrogen, carbon, nitrogen, and so on. Each of these elements is surrounded by space. If they weren't, they would be indistinguishable from each other. Which leads to the significance of space as it pertains to our life.

Space is the one ever-present constant that surrounds everything. Space separates the stars and planets, and makes one finger on our hand distinguishable from the next. And it also separates the molecules that make up seemingly solid objects, like steel and concrete. There is also space between every cell in our bodies and between all components of an atom. Everything is composed of space. If space were removed from anything, all that would remain is a lifeless blob of nothing. If there was no space inside our lungs, we couldn't draw a breath. If there was no space surrounding our heart, it couldn't beat and pump our blood. Space is an ever-present field of energy.

Everything that ever was, and everything that ever will be, must originate from the space surrounding it. A child was not placed into the womb as completely developed. It grew from a few tiny cells from each parent, combining and then multiplying. And where did those cells originate, and the ones those cells came from, and on and on into infinity? Likewise, everything that ever was or ever will be will die, returning to the space from where it originated.

I like to think of space in terms of silence, since they share essentially the same characteristics, and silence is a little more discernible to us than space. To see what I mean, sit alone for a few minutes in a quiet place, and listen to the silence around you. Do you notice the little noises that come and go? Listen. Soon you will hear little things: the refrigerator starting up, the air conditioner turning on, a car driving by. But before you heard the sound, there was silence. When the sound stopped being made, again, silence.

The sound came from somewhere, and when it stopped, it again went somewhere. You couldn't see the noise, but you know it was there. Where does it come from? Where does it go? What is it made up of? Silence is like space, in that noises come from silence and return to silence, just like every material object comes from space and returns to space. Space is the backdrop of our existence, and everything we understand with our senses is nothing more than our mental projections onto this infinite backdrop.

We have all heard the phrase, "Silence is golden." That little phrase is pretty significant. It can be understood that silence is the only language God speaks. In a sense, it's a universal language; all living things can speak and understand it fluently. This is also why a moment of silence is often regarded as the highest form of honor one can bestow.

As all of life, and even the material things we have, come and go, silence—or space—is the one constant. This is the one infinite presence that has always been and always will be. This is God. Silence cannot be produced in the mind. Nothing can make silence. Silence just *is*. It exists before anything. Silence is the stillness we belong to and where we originate.

Thinking in terms of space, we have to think of just how much space there is. Physicists realize all things are made up of a sort of energy, and everything appears to be in a constant state of vibration. Physicists believe all things are made of the most miniscule of particles, separated by space. They tell us there is space between every cell in our bodies, and since the average body is made up of nearly 100 trillion cells, with space separating each one, it is obvious we are actually made almost completely out of space. This space, which makes us who we are, is full of life energy. This Energy is what makes up all things. This is God!

Understanding this concept of space and knowing the connection we all share is essential in the evolution of our consciousness. It is this fundamental understanding that has eluded the majority of humankind since our creation. Human beings have one characteristic that distinguishes us from any other living thing: our ability to think intellectually. This ability would appear to be very beneficial and provide us with quite an advantage over the other living things of the world. But as history shows us, the human mind can be a very dangerous and destructive force when used in the wrong way. The history of humankind is one of violence and fear. Instead of harnessing our divine nature, we have opted more often to use our minds to control our thoughts rather than live in the present moment (becoming conscious). This is the reason we suffer today.

Since we are all made from the same space that makes up everything, that includes that which we label as God. This space is who we are fundamentally. However, when we were created, we were designed to have a functioning mind. The purpose of this mind is to navigate the world around us. Unfortunately, we have allowed this mind to dominate our lives. We have lost sight of the present moment, our connection to God. We were not given owner's manuals on how to survive in this world, or what or who we truly are or where we have come from. As humankind first began to walk on this planet, we had to sort of "wing it" to find out for ourselves all the answers of the universe. Even after all the time we have had to figure things out, we are still far from becoming an "awakened" species, which we are destined to become.

The history of the human race is certainly one of suffering. But we must understand there is a purpose for it all. It is all in divine order. Even the senseless barbaric acts we have inflicted on one another throughout the ages are part of the perfection of it all. Understanding our history is very helpful in understanding where we, as a species, have come from and are destined to go. In chapter 3 I discuss a brief overview of our history and what has brought us to the world we experience today.

# 3

---

## A Brief History

*The history of humanity is one that we may one day realize our
insanity and long for something far greater than what
we have come to know.*

When the first humans began to walk the earth, we
were hardly distinguishable from any other animals
that existed at the time. We were a primitive species.
There was no language and no society. Over time, however, humans
began to communicate, first with hand signals, probably some
grunts and groans, and then by drawing pictures. Spoken language
soon followed, making life much easier by allowing people to
communicate to each other different ways of surviving in the world.
As communication flourished, man began to settle into tribes and
communities. Leaders were chosen to be the voices of the groups, to
make command decisions, and to enforce rules. This became a major
role in our evolvement into a civilized society.

In the beginning, hunting and gathering were the ways of feeding
and providing for a particular group. But when communities and
tribes formed, farming became the primary source of food, allowing
for more jobs to be done within the confines of the community.

Due to the variety of different jobs being done within the
community, not everyone was able to go out and hunt and gather

food, so trading markets developed. This led to the development of a currency system, which we still use today. When currency emerged, it became a way for everyone to buy needed food and supplies. They no longer had to go out and get it on their own. Currency became a major point of influence as we evolved. With the origin of currency, as well as having a ruling entity, the formation of a class system of civilization began to emerge.

Also during the early portion of humankind's existence, people probably wondered who they really were and where they all came from. The sun and moon in the sky, and all the stars, where looked upon with reverence and worshipped. It was apparent, even back then, that there had to be something more, some great power that created life. The formation of villages provided people the ability to share ideas of a creating force. The belief in one supreme deity would soon arise, and monotheism would emerge, thereafter. These ideas were the beginning of our modern-day religions.

But the truth about our existence was rarely known throughout human evolvement. Even today it remains unnoticed to most. Throughout the ages, religion has tried to make sense of what we are and where we come from, but it has missed the mark for the most part. There were, however, several notable people throughout history who did understand the truth and realized their connection to the divine. People like the Buddha and Jesus Christ are the most notable of these early "knowers." These people had an understanding of life far beyond what most realized or could even fathom.

Kings and rulers began to see the strong devotion people put into their early religious beliefs. It wasn't long before the rulers began to adopt the religions, as well. The ruler then seemed to have a connection to the divine within their nations. Throughout history, there were the Jesuses and Buddhas who spoke truths and preached ideas the majority of people didn't quite understand.

People who lacked the capacity to comprehend the true meanings of these teachings manipulated the words and ideas throughout the years. Rulers and "holy" people have converted the truth into something they could understand. They often used a person's devotion to a particular religion as a tool to harness control over their people. Since there was no hard evidence of a supreme God, it became quite easy for leaders with agendas to instill fear in the masses through the use of their religious beliefs. The emergence of a god with the mind-set and emotional capacity of a human being is a prime example of what could come from a people who lacked the understanding of what is real.

Rulers learned making a god that would reward the good and seek justice for indiscretions was an effective way to rule. But the judgments of these "wrongdoings" were nothing more than opinions, often loosely based on religious teachings. If the people didn't want to follow the orders of a human king, having a vengeful god or rulers who made themselves into deities would be a way of making them follow the rules.

Now, a society of classes had taken hold out of the distribution of wealth and the role each member of society played. The kings having direct contact with God in most cases, makes it is easy to see how large-scale corruption and greed began. The lowest classes were poorly educated and worked long and hard to get things they needed. The middle classes worked hard but were afforded a few more luxuries than the lower class. The elites lived extravagant lifestyles. They didn't have to work that hard, because the other classes worked and provided for their needs. Currency was always more abundant in the higher class, while the lower and middle classes struggled to earn what they needed. Sounds strikingly similar to our modern-day society, does it not?

It can be argued that with poverty comes lack of education. And with lack of education comes a class of society that may not have the knowledge necessary to challenge a corrupt ruler or government, allowing for agendas to be fulfilled. In the early centuries of humankind, people were born into and remained in the class their parents belonged to. There was no upward mobility. No one was ever there to tell a small child he or she could be a ruler someday, if the child worked and sacrificed enough. It was uncommon to think beyond the societal barrier established by the leaders. Everyone was essentially destined to his or her fate from birth. It's amazing how that has barely changed throughout history.

It is more common today, however, for people to think outside the isolated mind they were raised to have, but this is still very rare. People born into poverty today rarely go on to live a better life than their parents had, simply because of the mind-set passed from generation to generation. Not understanding our own divinity keeps people locked into what they were taught by parents who struggled to live a mediocre life and never understood life is what we make of it.

It is no coincidence that the poorest children often receive the least amount of education. It is a flawed mentality and must change. Teaching our children that they are more than just poor kids from a poor family, and that each of us has the same divine ability as everyone else, is where change will begin to take shape on a global level.

## Religion

*The populace think that your rejection of popular standards is a rejection of all standard, and mere antinomianism; and the bold sensualist will use the name of philosophy to gild his crimes. But the law of consciousness abides.*
*—Ralph Waldo Emerson*

Religion became crucial to life in the early centuries and its influence continues into our modern world. Religion has been the standard-bearer of morality throughout the years. Since organized religion began, it established its laws and rules according to the doctrine of each particular belief. Even today, the major religions of the world—Christianity, Islam, and Judaism—have their own ideas of what is right and what is wrong based on their respective belief systems.

The laws enforced in each region of the world practicing a particular religion are based on these same beliefs. Christianity teaches that living with a partner before marriage is a sin, but it happens more often than not in this country. Most religions view homosexuality as going against what their god wants, which is nothing more than an opinion. In many Islamic beliefs, women are not held as equal to a man. Those are just a few of their beliefs.

Because not all religions believe in the same set of principles and values, it is impossible for everyone to agree on one particular way of thinking. The problem is many of these laws and ideas contradict what another religion may teach. They also restrict many of the freedoms we should have as people. They are nothing more than beliefs and opinions held by a certain group of people.

Of course, not everyone of a particular religion believes in the strictest of these laws. As Archbishop Desmond Tutu is quoted as saying,

> I can't for the life of me imagine that God will say, "I will punish you because you are black, you should have been white; I will punish you because you are a woman, you should have been born a man; I will punish you because you are homosexual, you ought to have been heterosexual." I can't for the life of me believe that is how God sees things.

In the modern Western world, we are told we are free, but how free are we really? Many of the opinion-based, outdated beliefs of the past are simply not relevant in today's world, and they cause restrictions and divisions to run rampant.

Laws that should be meant for people's safety have become rules that limit people's freedoms and isolate nonbelievers and those who don't practice that particular set of religious teachings. Laws have begun to govern ethical, opinion-based issues. Judgment and outcome on these issues come from other humans, whose opinions can be swayed in any circumstance to fit the mold of what those in judgment may believe or want to impose. This is a problem, since many people today do not practice a specific religion or don't agree with the premise of any particular ideology.

The number of people who believe in and practice religion consistently today is far less than even a few decades ago. Most people do believe in a supreme being, many believe in a god, but very few people ever think to look beyond the teachings of our ancestors. Many more simply don't know what to believe, so they just follow along with what their parents taught them.

Each religious group wants to be the one "true" religion. Thus conflict arises and wars begin, all in the name of the one true god. And a rationalization for going to war is all too often misleading when a religious undertone is used as justification to a people who have been taught a particular set of beliefs.

Controlling people through fear became common practice in the early days of modern religion and continues today. What began as the belief in the all-powerful God was manipulated and used to achieve power and acquire wealth. Rules and laws have transpired through the use of religion, and the use of these opinion-based ideals are being imposed onto the people, regardless of any differing personal beliefs. Instead of merely providing for the protection and safety of the people, these laws began to punish based on specific religious ideologies.

People can revolt against a ruler who oversteps authority, but who is to question the word of God? Most of the laws we have today are based on the religious beliefs of our ancestors. And foreign relations of almost every country base their policies on this predominantly religious background, which attributes to differences of opinion on many scales, as well as conflict.

For centuries, wars have been fought with the pretext of a religious notion tied to them. "Believe in *my* God or suffer the wrath, for it is God's will," was the mind-set. Whether the leaders of the warring nations ever believed in the religious rhetoric was irrelevant. It was all the justification and leverage they needed to win over the minds of the people they led into battles to attain the land and riches they sought.

Religion, in and of itself, is not to blame. But the narrow-minded way in which religion has been bastardized throughout the years has made it more of a hindrance than a help in raising people above the violence and oppression that have plagued humankind from the beginning. Practicing a particular religion may be the way some people express themselves, but pushing personal beliefs onto others to the extent of violence and hatred is completely senseless. It only furthers the restriction of our spiritual expansion as a species.

Many people feel that without religion, the world would become immoral, and chaos would ensue. But look at the state of the world today. There are wars raging all across the globe, most with some religious ideological implication. People are killing each other. Drug use and violence on our streets run rampant. All this occurs as people have become oblivious to the fact we have a divine connection to each other. These things are nothing new. They have been the norm for centuries.

Religion, for some, may be a way of coping and trying to make sense of what we do not understand. But religion may not be the answer for everyone. We have put all our faith into something that hasn't provided much toward becoming a peaceful world. The basic idea of religion was created with good intentions, I believe, and many great ideas and teachings have risen from the various world religions throughout history.

But many aspects of religion have been taken far from their original course and even misconstrued. The teachings and philosophies of religions are as varied and opinion based as each person who teaches it. Take the Bible for example. Give the book to ten practicing Christian leaders of different denominations, and each will interpret it differently. From fundamentalists to more contemporary practices, each allows for varying degrees of tolerance. Getting everyone to agree on any particular set of beliefs is impossible.

We do not need a religion or belief system to tell us what is right and what is wrong. So the idea of pushing certain beliefs onto everyone equally is asinine. Albert Einstein is quoted as saying, "If people are good only because they fear punishment and hope for reward then we are a sorry lot indeed." Having faith in a god and practicing religion may be a noble practice, but imposing certain ideas and beliefs onto others is an uphill battle that will always result in conflict. We don't need any more reasons to hate each other. We need more love and compassion, and for that to happen, it doesn't matter what set of beliefs we have. Tolerance and acceptance are the only ways to peaceably move forward.

Having a mind to think freely is not an accident. If God is our creator, and if he is perfect, as is the teachings of every religion I am aware of, he would certainly understand a little skepticism and truth seeking. We all have the ability to think and reason for ourselves. Until we begin to really examine what we have been taught, we will remain in the position we have always been, hoping and praying for a better life, instead of making the necessary adjustments each of us has the ability to make. We are each capable of taking full responsibility for our own lives, and until we do so, there will be suffering. Our history is a violent one, but it was completely necessary for the progression of our consciousness. Understanding this is necessary to transcend the madness and move toward a peaceful existence.

## A Violent World

*The barbaric and ruthless acts of our history have a divine purpose that we may one day unite and see beyond our limited vision of existence.*

The universe has been wrought with violence since its inception. The big bang, which brought us the universe we have today, was the initial act of violence. The earth, as it is, was formed when rock and iron slammed into each other and heated to unimaginable temperatures. Violent volcanoes, earthquakes, hurricanes, and ice storms in the early days were also essential in creating a habitable planet.

Similarly, living things must rely on other living things as sustenance to survive. There is a hierarchy of dominance called the food chain. Every living thing is a part of this food chain, and being at the top is imperative if we expect to live for any length of time. So clearly, some of the violence is necessary for our existence. Human beings, with our limited physical defense mechanisms, were not much competition to larger animals and pack animals, like the wolf, in our early days. But when humans were able to use our most valuable weapons—our brains—to harness the power and usefulness of fire, it became one of the most essential elements in the evolution of our species.

Humankind made its early tools and weapons out of wood and stone, and eventually out of bronze. But it wasn't until the discovery of iron that we really began to create. Iron was much more durable than any of the other materials in use. The use of iron, though it advanced humankind in many ways, also revolutionized weaponry and brought about an even bloodier and more violent era. It was the early Chinese who created a weapon that to this day has caused a significantly large number of deaths. As these ancient Chinese alchemists worked to invent a chemical that would bring about eternal life, they ended up accidentally creating gunpowder. With the use of these weapons, coupled with a mind that does not realize our connection to each other, humankind has caused millions upon millions of deaths and brought about violence on an unimaginable scale.

Human beings have taken on an us versus them mentality over the centuries. We perceive other humans to be the enemy. Initially, it was a fight for food and water supplies, which progressed into a fight for power and monetary gain. A belief in our separateness from each other has turned into the fear-based mind-set we see today. The cohesion that must exist in order to evolve into a more unified species has been replaced with a fear of others. Too often, we look at others with preconceived ideas that another person has more than we do or will even take what we have if we are not careful. This type of thinking has created divisiveness and contributes to the problems we have in our world today.

Humanity must unite if we are to coexist on this planet. Otherwise, the fear-based mind-set of us versus them will cause us to completely destroy each other and most likely, the planet in the process. Still, as hard as it is to believe, all the seeming madness in our history has a purpose. It is necessary for the evolution of human consciousness. Regardless of our personal beliefs of how we wish the world would be, our minds may never comprehend the intricate design of this perfect existence, which God has created. There is no evil force in conflict with the good of the universe. There is only a flawed mind-set that needs correcting.

# Evil

*There is nothing in this world that is not a direct reflection of the images of our mind, which we continuously send forth to the perfection of Infinity.*

Some say an evil entity is the cause of all the seemingly bad things we endure. But if you think about that for a second, you will wonder if God is infinite, how can evil and God coexist? It's simply not possible. For them both to exist, one would have to know the other, and limitations would have to be made. We already know Infinity (God) cannot be limited. If God is infinite perfection, evil can only be a creation of that perfection. Only the human mind can make such a distinction, since the mind is the only way of seeing anything other than the perfection of infinity.

"Evil" is a word humans have come up with to make sense of these so-called bad things in the world. Using such a word does nothing more than take away the responsibilities we should have for our own lives and placing them onto some imaginary entity. As I discuss a little later, infinity is perfection, God is infinite, and infinity is not divisible, so nothing exists that is not a part of God's perfection. The word "evil," in and of itself, is subjective in nature. It is impossible for every single living being to agree on what is evil and what is not.

Looking out into nature, it is inconceivable to imagine a squirrel blaming some evil entity for the forest fire that burned down the tree where it lived. I doubt the ram on a mountain cliff, when challenged for dominance, believes its challenger is possessed by an evil being. I find it hard to imagine the grasslands could waste a thought blaming a human for starting the brush fire that wiped out thousands of acres. The world revolves, things happen, and people and events create change. Blaming anything that occurs on some evil presence would impose limitation onto a limitless God. It just doesn't make sense.

When we stop placing blame for our perceived problems on some external evil entity, we are then in a position to take responsibility for our lives. From this position, we have the ability to rectify the situation without relying on a judgmental God, who may or may not assist us, given His judgment of our thoughts and actions preceding the problem. When we know anything bad in the world is a creation of the images made by the human mind, we can move forward with the knowledge of self-determinate greatness, knowing full well we have all the power and love to create the world we each desire to inhabit. We then have the understanding that every other being we encounter is here for our spiritual advancement. Transcend the limitations of the senses, transcend the limitations of the mind, and see with new eyes the enlightenment that is our divine purpose. Our existence is perfect. The universe is perfect. It cannot be otherwise.

# Imperfection

*See beyond the limitations of your mind and
embrace your divine presence.*

Imperfection is a creation of the mind. The question now is if
Infinity is perfect, how can we, as humans, not be perfect as well?
The answer to the question is that we indeed are perfect, as I've
previously stated, and we are here for Infinity to realize its own
existence. With our human mind, we perceive ourselves as not
being perfect, because the mind is a part of this physical body.
When the body dies, so does the mind. But *who* we are cannot die.
What we are fundamentally is a perfect creation of a perfect God,
making us perfection as well.

This is a prime example of a paradox—and a brief explanation
for our existence. We were created with a functioning mind to realize
there is something out there that is infinite, which is oneness, which
is pure love. God created us so we can realize His existence. All our
seeming imperfections are nothing more than judgments created
by our minds. Beneath our humanly flaws, however, is a divine
perfection that radiates in all creation. What we see as imperfection
is nothing more than our own judgment about a specific thought.

Throughout our lifetimes, and throughout history, labels have
been placed on everything to help us try to understand things better.
Labels of bad and good, right and wrong have been placed on nearly
every circumstance or situation we have encountered. We have been
raised to believe that certain things, ideas, and people are bad or
good. But good and bad are subjective. What one person considers
good another may consider bad. The foundation for these judgments
is based on our individual lives and the way each of us was taught to
think. These judgments can exist only within the mind.

In the book of Genesis, it says God created everything, and
everything God created was good (perfect). So how could anything
be otherwise? How could perfection spawn imperfection, unless it

was designed for that specific reason? With perfection, there can be no such thing as imperfection.

Human beings are indeed perfect, but the human mind believes anything falling short of our ideal image of ourselves, or the world around us, is less than perfect. Not understanding the purpose of any given circumstance or event has led people to label certain situations as good or bad. Somehow, the word "perfect" has become synonymous with being good. But with Infinity, which knows only perfection, perfect and imperfect simply cannot coexist. They are completely conflicting ideas. They are nothing more than subjective thought, an opinion. All of the infinite space of Energy, which creates and sustains everything we know to be our reality, is perfect, regardless of how we interpret it with our minds.

# 4

## *Infinity*

*The infinity of space is what distinguishes us from each other,
but it is also the connection we all share.*

When you look out into space and try to comprehend the vastness that lies beyond even what our own imagination can create, it all seems surreal. The Bible tells us God is the Alpha and the Omega, the beginning and the end, and this idea remains true to the beliefs of many. But where is the beginning or the end?

God, Infinity, and Space are the same thing: the creator of all life; it is the energy that sustains life. So why would God create anything if He is already infinite and would already contain everything? The answer to that is because God does not have a mind like we do and does not think like a human being; He has no reason to. God did not create us in His image, because God has no particular image; God is everything! He does not experience emotion in a human sense, and it is impossible to describe God in human words, because no such words exist. And even if there were such words, we would not be able to understand the meaning with our limited human intellect.

We, as human beings, cannot grasp this concept, so we created for ourselves a god with human-like characteristics. The closest word to "God" I can come up with in English is "infinity."

This brings us to the purpose of our creation. What reason would infinite space have to create anything? But think about the question. Infinity is *all* encompassing, as I have suggested, which could not leave out anything.

Ask yourself this: How could something infinite, which cannot be separate or distinct from anything else, know anything about itself? Infinity does not have a mind to think with, like we do. After all, how could it? Having a mind that thinks would provide the ability to recognize something that isn't. But as we have already discussed, Infinity is all encompassing; there is nothing that it is not. Therefore, Infinity would have to create something with the ability to recognize itself. And there is only one creation with that ability: the human mind.

Humans are designed to have a functioning mind, but that is not who we are. This independent mind has the ability to navigate the world we live in, but it cannot see beyond the physical forms that surround it or the present moment in which we exist. We all have the ability to connect to this infinite Space, or God, at will. However, from the earliest days of humankind, we have lost sight of this connection and reverted to the only thing that seemed real to us, which is the human mind. Thus began the suffering we endure to this day.

## *Now*

*Now is all there ever has been, all there is presently,
and all that will ever be.*

We all have within ourselves a connection to our divine nature, or God. We have all been created by something infinitely perfect and are, therefore, a part of this perfection. Over the course of our time in human form, however, we have lost sight of this connection. We have turned our lives over to a mind that can create nothing for itself.

This (human) mind that can think only in terms of past experiences or future desires. The mind does not exist in the present moment. The only thing that exists in the present moment is our conscious mind, which is our connection to God.

The present moment contains all of life. Nothing exists that isn't in this moment right now. Every thought you have is either a memory of the past, which has come and gone already, or a vision of the future, which does not yet exist. There is nothing that has ever happened, or will ever happen, that won't occur right now, in the present moment, which I will elaborate on when I discuss the concept of time. The present moment is where the stillness of space and silence reside. It is the only time that has ever been and is the only thing that is real. Something that happened a second ago is in the past and viewed by the mind as a memory. Something that will happen one second from now is only viewed by the mind as something that has not yet happened. Understanding our concept of time may make this topic a little easier to follow.

## Linear Time

*Time is nothing more than an instrument used to
gauge the limitations of our mind.*

Time is a tool used only by human beings. No other living thing wears a watch or needs a clock to tell them what they need to do or where they need to go. Time does not exist outside our limited ability to think. The creation of linear time was developed by people to help make sense of this world. We watch as our bodies age and the world around us changes, and we are tricked into believing time has actually passed. The belief of time as reality is deceiving.

Think about the essence of time as it relates to the universe. We live our life in roughly eighty years or so. But how does 80 years compare to the 13.5 billion years the universe has existed, or the 13.5

billion years before our universe was formed, and on and on into infinity? We could have lived nearly 170 million lifetimes since our current universe began! If we keep looking at time in that sense, we are going to have to constantly look at what came before that, and before that, and so on. There is no end.

This may be a little difficult to follow, since we use time for almost everything we do. We need to wake up on time to get to work, we need to be on time to a doctor's appointment, and so on. But it is very important to realize nothing ever happens at any other time than now, the present moment. Every moment of our life happens in the present moment. That time when you were six years old and you fell off your bicycle happened in the present moment, did it not? Were you not present in that moment? Our conscious mind is the same as it has always been, and it has always been constant and present in this moment. When we become present in this moment, we are just as present as we have ever been or will ever be.

With linear time, we have a past, a present, and a future. Two of these are simply not a possibility in the scope of infinity. There is no beginning and no end. So where would a past or a future fit into an indefinite time scheme? It doesn't. The only time there has ever been and will ever be is right now! This present moment is all there is. Our past and our vision of our future are nothing more than that—a vision, or an illusion, in our mind, if you will. One can never go back to a time in the past. The only thing we have is a memory of an event, and our memories are stored in our ego-based (human) mind. Memories are irrelevant outside the dimensions of physical form.

Take, for example, a tree. A tree goes though the stages of its life without needing to know what time it is. A tree knows better than to question environmental changes or any other occurrence. It simply accepts life as it comes. This is true for all of nature. There is no need for a clock in nature. Life just goes on. Of course, the sun rises and sets, and the physical condition of our body changes. But everything that will ever happen, or has already happened, happens right now in this moment. We are deceived by seeing changes and believing they happened at a time other than right now. Life is not a moving picture; it is a sequence of still photographs taken all at once.

The fact that we can remember certain times in our past is the ability of our mind to recall events that have occurred. It still remains that we were just as present at the moment of its occurrence as we are in this moment; there was no other moment! Having a past is important, as long as we can learn from it. But clinging to our past will lead to suffering, because it takes us out of the present moment, the only time there is. The present hasn't changed; only the circumstances we perceive to be real have been altered. Understanding that linear time is not real is not an easy concept to comprehend, since we are never taught differently. It is important, however, to be aware of this. We were born *now*, we live *now*, and we will die *now*. True reality never changes.

Everything our senses can detect is in a constant state of change, so what is it that we can say never changes? All that we know will one day cease to be. All of life, all material things, this earth, and the sun will one day go away. Everything physical is in a constant state of transformation from existence to nonexistence. Our bodies are continuously changing, and material things eventually decompose or erode away. So what is it that never changes?

## What Is Real?

> That is real which never changes.
> —Nisargadatta Maharaj

So what is it that is real and does not change? First of all, it may be easier to understand what *does* change. Looking around, we may notice everything in the universe changes at some point. On earth, nature is always going through stages of life, death, and rebirth. Metal rusts, rocks erode, and flowers wilt and decay back into the ground. But the one constant, which I have previously mentioned, is space. Space does not change and has never changed in all of eternity. And space resides in the present moment.

Would it be a comfort or a horror to know everything we encounter with our senses is nothing more than an illusion, a projection into physical form of something our mind conceived? If your response was anything other than comfort, you may be in for a shock. You will most likely wonder, *How can it be an illusion when I can touch, taste, smell, hear, and see all that is around me?* The answer is not simple. What I can say is this: all that is real never changes.

So everything we can see, touch, taste, and smell is not real? It must be understood that all the things we can experience with the senses are manifestations of the images we project in our mind. They are nothing more than illusions. What we understand to be tangible things will all one day cease to be, lost in the infinity of Space. Our human minds will be gone eventually, and all that will remain is the ever-present conscious mind, our soul-for lack of better terms; everything else is transient. As I have previously explained, our mind is only capable of seeing past events, and we want future events. We all understand the past to be a place in time that has already come and gone, but what about the desires we have for the future? Where are they right now? Where can they be? There is no other time than right now, and nothing exists that isn't in this moment. So where else could the fulfillment of our desires reside?

We have a human mind with limited capabilities. This mind is an instrument used to navigate our way around the world in which we exist. But this mind cannot stretch past the limits of what we individually have come to know. It is not possible to know and understand our limitless Creator with the mind alone. Our thinking mind, as great as it is, simply is not capable of comprehending the extent of our existence. We interpret the world around us based on the use of our five senses, which are nothing more than an extension of our brain. And the brain is a part of our physical body, which is worldly. This means it is subject to change, making it not real in terms of infinity. The human mind, referred to as the ego in a spiritual context, is nothing more than our limited, worldly mind. In trying to make sense of the things it does not understand, the mind has created its own version of reality. The mind has created its own world, so to speak, and this world is limited by the depth of our human intelligence and subject to the judgments and polarity of our thoughts. This is the birth of the ego, and the ego has left us with a very distorted view about what is real.

# The Witness

*Life is fully lived only when we realize that our truest self is beyond the illusion of the senses.*

Have you ever noticed yourself behaving in a certain way or experiencing a certain emotion? Have you ever been able to sit back and watch your reaction as certain events unfolded? Who notices your experiences in those situations? Who watches you, in peaceful observation, while your entire body and mind fill with anger or any other passionate emotion?

We have all experienced this at some point, but very few people stop to consider what is actually taking place. Take a second to contemplate this. If your body and mind are filled to the brim with emotion, yet something else is sitting idly by, observing the whole event, whom or what is doing the observing? The observer is your conscious mind. We all have one; it is who we truly are. This is our divine connection to God. This is the only part of us that never changes, the only part of us that is real, and the part that was never born and will never die. This is sometimes referred to as the witness.

We can alleviate negative feelings by allowing the witness to preside. When I refer to the witness, I mean that part of us that can sit idly by and watch as our body and mind are consumed by emotions or thoughts. When we are angry with our spouse for not following through on a promise, or for any other reason, we can just sit back and observe the feelings we have about the situation. We will notice there is another part of who we are, separate from the emotion, that can actually witness the situation as it unfolds.

When we allow ourselves to be this witness, the emotions don't have the same effect. It's almost as if we are outside our body, watching what is happening. When we are in this state, we are actually being present in the moment. We are connected to that infinitely creative Space. We can know within ourselves why we feel the way we feel, or what caused the emotion to surface, and the solution will come from deep within with a profound understanding. When we take ourselves out of the situation and into the present moment, we will soon feel the emotions fade away, and a sense of peace will emerge.

The position of being the witness is very helpful in any situation, and it is accessible at any time. When we experience circumstances in which we don't feel comfortable, or a situation we simply don't want to be in, allow the witness to observe. Soon the lesson to be learned will become apparent.

It is very important to remember, however, that life is constantly flowing, and being where we are is exactly where we are supposed to be. Understand that desiring anything that is not in this moment is a form of resistance to what is. Everything is the way it is supposed to be. There is a lesson in this moment, and resisting what is happening now will only cause suffering. We need to make it a habit to remind ourselves this moment is all there ever is, and whatever is happening is in divine order.

When you are in the middle of rush-hour traffic after a long day, and all you want is to be home, sit back and allow the witness to observe the situation. Knowing we have no control over what is happening at this moment means we can allow ourselves to witness what is taking place. Accept it! Feel the peace of accepting the situation as we disconnect from our mind and reconnect to God. Many spiritual teachers refer to this as surrendering, or just allowing what is happening to be the way it is without judgment. If you have the ability to change the circumstances in a more favorable way, do so. If not, accept what is and find the peace of the present moment.

If you have never experienced the witness I am referring to, or if you don't believe such an observer exists within you, catch yourself the next time you feel any particular emotion. Watch how you can become a witness to what is taking place within your body and your mind. You can observe the physical changes in your body, such as an increased heart rate, muscles tense, and quicker, shallower breathing. You can also observe your mind as it thinks its way around the topic. You can actually watch as the emotion consumes your body and mind. Anger, fear, or any other negative emotion can be felt physically. These emotions may even be as debilitating as any form of illness or disease, but there is always that peace, that presence within, that can sit back, impartial to the events taking place. This is the witness. We all have it. It is who we truly are; it is our conscious mind. It just needs to be understood. I can promise you this much, though. If you are able to witness yourself while your body and mind are consumed in deeply negative emotion, observing and not casting any judgments toward how you feel, you will soon begin to watch the feeling fade away. This is the power you have by connecting to the Infinite. Having and experiencing emotions are inevitable parts of being human, but it is impossible not to experience peace when we are fully present in the moment.

## Freewill

*We are at every moment free to make a choice, but we can never understand with our minds that which we have not yet learned.*

How are we able to use our minds at will while still having a distinct, divine consciousness? With the use of our human minds, we have been given the ability to hold opposing ideas. We are able to see a distinction between the infinite energy of Creation and our physical presence. The perfection of Infinity cannot hold an opposing idea, because it is impossible for perfection to be separate from itself. To do so would create limitation, therefore, creating imperfection.

This may be starting to sound a little redundant, but it needs to be understood. What has been created is a being with the ability to hold opposing ideas (humans), allowing one of those ideas to see the perfection of Infinity and the other to see the seemingly limited physical world. How we have chosen to use the latter is a choice each of us makes every second of the day, but understanding the former is not something we are usually taught. We have allowed ourselves to believe we are separate from what we truly are, and we have begun to create our version of what we think is real. We have allowed our human mind to create limitations. And when we think only with our human minds, we forget limitations cannot exist in the ultimate scheme of reality.

What we think, Infinity reflects back to us. Infinity cannot make judgment calls. God cannot decide which thought he is going to entertain and which he is not. Therefore, each of our thoughts is a request to Infinity. This is where our thoughts become the determining factor in what we experience every day.

As I mentioned before, Infinity, Space, or God does not have a mind and does not think. God doesn't need a mind when he is infinite, thus all knowing. Imagine Infinity to be a giant mirror. We all know how a mirror works; it reflects everything put in front of it. The same thing goes for God. God does not think, so God cannot cast judgment on anything. All our thoughts, which are made of nothing, are already in space. God already knows our thoughts, and since God is not judging our thoughts, they are simply reflected back to us. The judgment of good and bad are all determined by each of us, or as Shakespeare stated, "Nothing is either good or bad but thinking makes it so."

No one has ever seen a thought. A thought is not a tangible thing. The average person has about seventy thousand thoughts in a single day, and there is no way all those thoughts could fit inside even the biggest brain. So I venture to say thoughts are nothing more than space, which to bring the point home once again, is God. God doesn't judge our thoughts; He can't. All God can do is reflect our thoughts back to us and provide for us that which we think.

There are several phrases out there depicting this idea, including, "Thoughts become things," or, "You become what you think about."

Thoughts do indeed become things. When you have the thought, *I am upset,* you are sending that message to the Infinite. Reflected back to you are your feelings of being upset. Try this the next time you feel upset. Think, *I can be happy in any moment,* and allow yourself to smile; force yourself if you must. I promise the feeling of being upset will subside or at least become manageable. Because you changed the thoughts you are sending out, what is being reflected has changed. This works in all facets of life, as I will explain.

Nothing in this world existed without first being a thought. I can give you a hundred examples of how this works, but we will start out small. For example, early humans had a thought of, *I don't want to be cold anymore,* or, *I'm tired of eating raw meat.* Soon they discovered fire. As humans evolved into our modern world, someone thought, *I want to be able to turn on a machine and have access to nearly all of the information in the world at the touch of a button.* Then the Internet was developed. On and on it goes, even into our personal lives. We had a thought of getting a job, of having a car, of getting married. The entire process is nothing more than a collection of sequential thoughts. Before anything came into your life, you first had a thought—consciously or unconsciously—that you wanted a certain thing or person in your life. But you may say, "I don't have the house I want, or the job I want, or even the spouse I want." And this is where the proof lies.

The thoughts you think are reflected back to you, but you may not always send clear signals. When you think, *I really want to be an architect,* but consciously or subconsciously you think, *I want to be an architect, but I could never afford to go to college,* or, *I am not smart enough to be an architect.* These thoughts are also reflected back to you. When you think, *This is what I want my dream spouse to be like,* while thinking, *But I could never get anyone like that,* you will get what you think you can have. "What you think about is what expands," is what Dr. Wayne Dyer, in *There's a Spiritual Solution to Every Problem* (HarperCollins 2001), points out.

In *As a Man Thinketh* (1902), James Allen explains how each person creates his or her destiny. He writes, "Man is made or unmade by himself; in the armory of thought he forges the weapons by which he destroys himself; he also fashions heavenly mansions of joy and strength and peace."

Our mind can be as self-destructive or as lovingly creative as we choose to make it. The choice is always up to us. We limit our abilities to create for ourselves, because we have lost sight of the fact we are connected to Infinity, which already contains everything. Everything we can imagine, everything we may desire, already exists. It has to. Since there is no such thing as time, there is nowhere else it could be.

Most people are under the assumption they have to deal with life the way it is, that they must play the hand they were dealt. We spend most of our time wishing things, situations, and circumstances were different. One thing we must understand, however, is that Infinity must create and provide everything the human mind sends out to it. Infinity, in and of itself, simply cannot have any thoughts separate from the mind. Ernest Holmes, in his book *Creative Mind* (Wilder Publications 2010), wrote, "Wonderful as the Universal Mind is, it has no choice but to create whatever thought is given it; if it could contradict that thought, it would not be a unit, since this would be recognizing something outside itself."

As I said earlier, each thought we have is profoundly important. Tens of thousands of different thoughts flow through our minds in a single day. Each of these thoughts is much more powerful than most of us may realize.

I'm sure there are plenty of things you want out of life, such as material things, relationships, or a specific job. Most people I know, and the ones I see on a daily basis, are content. They are content to do what will get them by. But I know very few people who are genuinely happy with where they are in life. Most people think life is a struggle, that we have to work hard to get the things we want. But what if I told you it doesn't have to be that way? What if I said you could have anything you want with very little effort on your part? Well, I am here to tell you that is absolutely the case. This is not a fantasy or wishful thinking. What I am talking about is connecting to Infinity. As I established earlier, Infinity is all encompassing, and linear time doesn't really exist outside our minds, so everything that ever has been or ever will be must exist now. Time and space are infinite! Everything exists now, in the present moment.

This may sound ridiculous to many people, because we only see what we can interpret with our minds. But there is nothing real about our minds. The things we encounter with our senses are only a vision of a mind that will one day cease to exist. Who we are fundamentally is a divine presence. This divine presence is a part of perfection, a part of Infinity. That which we truly are was never born and will never die, but has always been.

As I have explained, every thought we think carries with it the potential to become a physical manifestation. When we have thoughts of, *I am struggling to get by. I'm never going to get past this,* Infinity will reflect, "You are struggling; you are never going to get past this." And the cycle continues. The way to change this is to change the way we think. Norman Vincent Peale said, "Change your thoughts and you change your world." It's such a simple notion yet quite profound. A simple thought can change the entire course of our lives.

When we have thoughts of lack, we are sending these thoughts into Infinity. Conscious thoughts such as, *I can never get out of debt, I can never find a compatible partner, I hate my job,* just to name a few, are the limiting thoughts we probably had at one point or another.

But in understanding how manifestation works, we can get an idea of why we are in certain situations. Realizing the power each of our thoughts has makes it quite apparent that we should take control over the thoughts we allow entering our minds. Napoleon Hill, in his book *Think and Grow Rich* (1937) wrote, "If you can conceive and believe you can achieve." Having an idea, *knowing* it will be manifested into physical form, and assuredly, it will be ours. The only real limitations to accessing our full potential come from our lack of knowing and our inability to understand our divinity.

## *Belief versus Knowing*

*To believe is to wish; to know is to allow.*

In regard to our thoughts, we must first distinguish between something we believe in and something we know to be true. A belief is an opinion with some doubt attached to it. Words like "hope" and "desire" are nothing more than beliefs. These words sound comforting but are actually riddled with suffering. When we hope or desire a specific thing to transpire, what we are actually doing is saying to Infinity that we don't feel we can achieve or arrive at the desired event; there is a doubt attached. These are conflicting messages, whether consciously or subconsciously, that we want a particular thing but don't feel capable of manifesting what we actually want. In doing this, we allow whichever thought is the most predominant to manifest itself. This is why it is important to distinguish between a knowing and a belief.

Knowing a certain thing, without a doubt, will ensure its manifestation. The key thing to remember is that with knowing there cannot be any doubt. Do not try to deceive yourself. Merely telling yourself you know a thing to be true when in fact you know it is not is like looking into a mirror and expecting to see some other face looking back at you. A good example is having money. Everyone wants to have enough money to buy the things they need, or even enough to buy the things they don't necessarily need, but fail to *know* money is abundant. We can tell ourselves and even others that we have money, and even wish for more of it. But if we don't *know* we have the ability to manifest money, it will not last. Looking into your bank account and seeing ten dollars but telling yourself there is ten million dollars isn't going to work. We have to know something to be the truth; it is not possible to deceive God.

Regardless of whether we actually have money or not, we can still attract it into our life. The easiest and most efficient way of doing this is to change the thoughts we think. Change your thoughts from, *I can't earn enough or save enough,* to, *The world is infinitely abundant. There is more than enough for all of us to share.* This concept works in virtually every walk of life. I could dedicate an entire book to this truth, but manifestation is not the sole purpose of what I am trying to accomplish. All I intend to relay is the fact we have great power with our thoughts when we learn to harness and focus them.

Words like "belief," "hope," and "desire," on the surface are very uplifting for most. But these words are deceiving, because they each elicit a slight hint of doubt. Doubt is the loophole to positive thinking. We can believe we are happy in our relationships, hope we will recover from an illness, or desire to be in a different job. But that doubt will remain in our thoughts. Just like the conscious messages we send, these subconscious thoughts, as they often are, are also being projected.

## Suffering

*We will continue to suffer, until we realize that we do not have to suffer anymore.*

—*Buddha*

A question may be raised. You know so-and-so and have never met a happier and more upbeat person. So how is it that person got cancer, or suffers so much? The answer is simple. It is impossible for anyone to know exactly how another person thinks. What we see or know of a person is only the side he or she shows us. Everyone has thoughts and ideas that only he or she deals with. It is also impossible for us to know the subconscious thoughts of others. Perhaps they don't even realize the thoughts they are sending out. A person can be as happy as can be on the surface, but if he or she harbors any doubts, bitterness, or anything else negative, without question, those thoughts will be reflected in the form of physical manifestations.

James Allen said, "The soul attracts that which it secretly harbors; that which it loves and that which it fears; it reaches the height of its cherished aspirations; it falls to the level of its unchastened desires—and circumstances are the means by which the soul receives its own." Whatever it is that you have inside will ultimately find its way to the surface in the form of a physical manifestation.

## How

*Disallow limitations, and never again feel lack.*

One of the most common words that may hinder our pursuit of obtaining the life we want for ourselves is the word "how." How do I get the things I want? I want to be successful and own five cars, but how can I, when I am completely broke? What fails to be realized is that Infinity is limitless. It says in the Bible, Matthew 7:7, "Ask and you shall receive; seek and you shall find; knock and the door will be opened to you." All you simply have to do is think the thoughts you wish to see manifested in the world, know there are no limitations, and God will do the rest. No effort required!

Now you're probably thinking, *If it were really that easy, why isn't everyone just thinking different thoughts?* The answer is most people have never heard this logic before, and the majority of those who have simply refuse to believe it. It sounds extremely farfetched when we have known nothing other than what we were taught until now.

Take, for example, many of the world's millionaires and billionaires. Do you think they have something special that you do not possess? Do you think God granted their abundance because they are superior human beings? No! These people just have the mind-set they will have the money and the fame, and limited thoughts were never sent out. We hear stories all the time of how someone came from poverty to become very successful and very wealthy. None of these people have anything you don't have. The only thing that makes them different are the thoughts they send to Infinity.

We should not choose to limit our minds or allow anyone else's influence to change the images we want for ourselves. We should not limit ourselves based on what we believe is our own limited destiny. We must discard our old ways of thinking. The old doesn't exist anymore, because, as Oliver Wendell Holmes once said, "Man's mind, stretched to a new idea, never returns to its original dimensions." Once you realize the truth, you will never go back to your old way of thinking.

When it comes to seeking the dreams we have for ourselves, we must remain focused. We cannot allow any other thoughts to enter our mind. James Allen wrote, "A man should conceive of a legitimate purpose in his heart, and set out to accomplish it. He should make this purpose the centralizing point of his thoughts." We can get whatever we want for ourselves—perhaps a new house, a mansion overlooking the ocean, a fulfilling relationship, or to travel the world. All of these are attainable. Our desires should never be limited based on what we think we know. We cannot concern ourselves with how we will attain things. Simply knowing we will manifest them is all the work we need to do.

Personal relationships, however, are different. We can desire a certain relationship, but we cannot desire a specific person. Each person has his or her own mind and path in life. We cannot pull anyone from his or her life path just to satisfy our desires. I discuss relationships in further detail a little later.

We have covered a lot about where we come from, what we are capable of, and what we are doing here. But let's explore our divine purpose a little further. What is the purpose of our being on this planet under these specific circumstances?

# 5

## Our Divine Purpose

*For we are all one in reality, and our separateness is nothing but a*
*necessary illusion in the plan by which the Universal Mind*
*seeks to know itself by becoming a thing.*
*—Uell S. Andersen*

Our ability to think independently from God serves a functioning role, but our ability to consciously connect to God in the present moment is our purpose for existing. We can live on this planet with the ability to use our senses and be a human being, with all of the suffering interlaced with moments of happiness. Or we can be a spiritual Being, where we know our connection to God and live a life of peace, in this present moment, while experiencing life in human form.

The truth is we were created to experience life in human form, living in our unified consciousness with God, transcending our thinking mind, and residing primarily in the present moment. In this form, we have the ability to experience life in a way not possible in the true realm of our existence. This is the purpose of evolving our minds from those of the Neanderthals, to our current state, and to the state our minds will one day become. With every generation, there is evolvement of our physical, mental, and even spiritual abilities. The reason for our progression is based on our ability to think, to desire the things we want that give us pleasure, and to adapt to a world more suitable for our needs and desires. As our consciousness grows, we experience a separation of our truest selves from the physical form that holds us here in this world.

Eckhart Tolle, in *A New Earth: Awakening to Your Life's Purpose* (Plume 2005), described the evolution of humankind. It started when we were single-cell organisms living in water. A thought of becoming something more allowed us to breath out of water and then to swim. Then there was a thought to crawl onto land and breath the air directly into our lungs, and then to stand and walk. This all came as the result of a thought. Over the course of millenniums, we have enhanced our abilities to manifest. Today you can hold a piece of plastic in the palm of your hand, push a couple of buttons, and send a message to virtually any place on the globe within seconds. We can talk to someone in another country live via video camera on our smartphones and computers, and we can take a jet to any continent in a matter of hours.

Our physical bodies, along with the advances in technology and medicine, have raised life expectancy from twenty or thirty years to where it is now common for people to live well into their eighties and some even past one hundred. It is also apparent by looking at people that our bodies have changed considerably over the years. When it was necessary to hunt and gather food, our bodies were much leaner. Today, the average size of a man is larger. He is generally less fit, because it isn't necessary for us to exert as much effort to get things we need anymore. The luxury comes at a price, however, with an increase in health issues. But it is still proof of the evolvement, or adaptation, of humankind to the environment, which is the result of our thinking over the ages.

The human body has not had to change considerably in overall appearance over the last few centuries. This is due to the fact humans have been able to create an environment that caters to our bodies. We have learned to use heating and cooling to avoid forcing our bodies to make drastic physical changes, which would normally be necessary to survive in different climates.

Spiritually, we are becoming more in tune with who we truly are. The old beliefs are being disproved and falling away, giving us the opportunity to advance the global consciousness even further. With the evolution of our consciousness, we will unite with humankind and all other life forms in ways never seen before. We will manifest, as a unified global consciousness, all we need to experience heaven here on earth.

This is not a fantasy or some inconceivable, far-off place. This is the opportunity we each have in this moment. The opportunity to accept the now, to access our divine consciousness, and to live from this place as our primary means of living will bring about heaven on earth for each of us. When enough people live in this way, we will all experience this as the normal way of life.

But first, we have to realize where we come from. Our history is vitally important in helping us advance. More important, though, we must understand who we truly are. By making the mistakes we made in our past, we are able to move ahead with better understanding, both individually and globally. Our individual consciousness will allow us to move at our own pace, but the global consciousness must evolve as well. When we allow our conscious mind to prevail on an individual level, the global changes will be automatic, and the consciousness of the universe will evolve. It is the only way forward. Realizing our divinity is the most important change we can make. This realization will unify all living things and create a more peaceful existence.

We have each been given a unique human mind, but this mind will never allow us to understand why anyone or anything else is a certain way. For us to think anything should be different from the way it is now is to question the perfection of our existence. We each have a divine purpose, and no one has a greater or smaller role to play. The pope is no more or less essential than the homeless person on the street corner. Just because we have perceived judgments about how people should be does not mean we can understand the perfection in all things. In the Bible, Luke 12:7, it says that every hair on our head has been accounted for. Why would anything as seemingly insignificant as that be accounted for but the role each of us is here to play not be?

The purpose of our existence is to create a world that has achieved the highest form of spiritual enlightenment. A world where there is no hatred or greed and where we all realize we are one, that there is truly a heaven on earth. Each of us at our core, in our soul, is a part of the Infinite. All our perceived problems are simply our human minds consuming our thoughts and believing we are separate from each other and God. When we are able to step out of our human, ego-based mind and allow our conscious mind to work, we will realize we are Infinity itself. Then we will begin to understand just how significant each of us truly is.

Since Infinity is not divisible, we must all be one. Every living thing shares a connection. We all originate from the same place and will all return there again. We are a part of something much larger, something incomprehensible to our human understanding. This Infinity cannot be defined or explained with mere intellect. The human mind will one day pass away. All our thoughts and memories will no longer exist. All that will remain is what we fundamentally are: pure consciousness. This is Infinity; this is our connection to our Creator. But there can be no distinction between the infinity within each of us, within our neighbor, or any other living thing. At our source, this does not only make us a part of God but also one with God.

The idea of "being" God is preposterous to the logic of most people. We have been taught throughout centuries that we are subjects of God, not equals. To think otherwise is blasphemous in the eyes of most religions and ridiculous to most people. But if we are a creation of the perfect God and our soul—for lack of better term—is a part of that perfection, how can we not be that which we are a part of? As thirteen-century Persian poet Rumi stated,

"You are not a drop of water in the ocean, you are the entire ocean in a single drop." We are Infinity, although we appear separate and distinct within this physical form. Every living thing is a part of the Infinite, regardless of the form it takes or the action it produces. We are all one. We are all God!

When we are able to connect with our source, Infinity, we are able to become creators of our own world. Before we arrived on earth, we were infinite. When we shed this body, we will return to what we were before, infinite. Our purpose in this world is to realize we are not separate from God. We are, in fact, one in the same.

# Part 2

# The Human Experience

# 6

## *Ego*

*The human mind, when given the opportunity to take control, will be our greatest adversary.*

I n part 2, we explore the ego and how it affects different aspects of our lives: our relationships to each other, the emotions we experience, and what these emotions mean. We, as human beings, are quite unique. No other living being has the ability to think the way we do. But along with this ability comes the drama involved in not understanding our divinity. "Drama" is probably the best word to describe the ego, the human mind that cannot see past physical form. In advancing on a spiritual path, it is vitally important to understand the ego and its ability, given the opportunity, to control us all. We have become our own worst enemy. Understanding this is essential to progress beyond our thinking mind and toward our conscious connection to God.

With the ability to think on levels unattainable to any other living thing, we have created a world suited toward obtaining all our desires. These desires originate from a place separate from what we truly are. Desires come from the human mind, and with this mind, comes a lot of drama and baggage, with potentially disastrous consequences. Differentiating between what is created by the mind (manifestations of egoic desires) from what is a part of our divine existence (that which is real) is essential in moving forward. Understanding our human experience as it relates to how we think and understand the relationships we experience will help us in evolving our consciousness.

The mind's incessant flow of thoughts is an affliction affecting all of humanity. Being born into this world with the ability to think independently from the infinite flow of Energy has caused us to think in worldly terms most of the time. Very few people today have the ability to stop the constant flow of thoughts, which barrage us at will, at any given moment. The only way they become recognized is when our mind selects a specific thought and then personalizes it.

By conducting a quick experiment, you can see for yourself that the flow of thoughts is virtually impossible to control without practice. Sit for a few minutes and allow your mind to think but not on anything in particular. Just let the thoughts flow. Now tell your mind to stop thinking. I'm sure it is quite apparent that you are unable to stop the flow of thoughts for more than a few seconds before a new one comes creeping in. Now focus your thoughts on a material object in the room, perhaps a pen or chair. Think only about this item, and think about it nonjudgmentally. It will not take long before foreign thoughts begin to pop into your mind, completely out of your control. You're thinking about the pen, when all of a sudden, a thought forms in your mind about a dream you had last night or what you want to have for dinner later. You didn't think that particular thought at that instant. It just came to you, and you chose to bring it into the forefront of your mind, perhaps even unwillingly or subconsciously, because your ego identified with it.

This demonstration shows how difficult it is to control the flow of thoughts. Only by selecting a particular thought and dwelling on it do we allow ourselves to make the thought our own. So what does this mean? Where do the thoughts come from, and what can be done about it?

The thoughts we have are part of a larger constant flow of thoughts projected by the collective whole of humanity. Thoughts that have been projected out to Infinity by all human minds are reflected to us. The only way to interrupt the formulation and personalization of these thoughts is to become present. To make it a little clearer, allow me elaborate on desire.

## Desire

*To desire anything has become human nature; to accept everything is always divine nature.*

Mara is the name of a mythical being often referred to by Buddhists as the demon of temptation, the being that constantly tempted the Buddha while he sat under the Bodhi tree, waiting for enlightenment. After achieving his "awakening," the Buddha understood that temptation is the cause of all suffering, and ridding ourselves of suffering is the only way to bring us all to this great awakening, or enlightenment.

Suffering is not only the experience of physical or emotional pain often associated with the word. In this context, it refers to anything that creates discomfort or disrupts the flow of life. When we humans have the ability to use our minds, it is more accurate to say our minds actually use us. Desires arise from our mind, which attaches itself to a specific thought and then craves the manifestation of that particular thought.

There are a number of reasons why we, as individuals, crave the specific things that cause our temptations. The cravings, or desires we have for a specific thing—such as a certain job, a material object, or a particular type of relationship—is based on our conditioned mind. This means because we have all been raised a certain way, the ideas and beliefs we grew up believing to be true and identifying with have forged our mind into its current state. Of course, I am speaking only of our human mind, or the egoic mind, here. For instance, we have all grown up to have particular tastes in food. We crave the food that gives us pleasure. We have also developed our own version of the "ideal" romantic partner, based again on our mental conditioning.

The reason we have allowed ourselves to be tempted by certain cravings is because we believe in some way the fulfillment of this craving will satisfy the ego. In turn, hopefully, it will free us from the cravings and ultimately stop the suffering.

The problem with allowing our minds to operate this way is no amount of satisfaction will ever completely free us from our desires. The ego is never satisfied! This is obvious if you look at any part of your life. There is nothing on this planet that will satisfy us completely for our entire lives. There will always be good times and bad times, good feelings and bad feelings, joy interspersed with suffering. The time between these polarities will vary from person to person.

Now we see the ego is at the root of our cravings, making it the base of all of our temptations and, therefore, the cause of our suffering. As Nisargadatta Maharaj stated, "Freedom from desire means this; the compulsion to satisfy is absent." As long as we allow our ego to control our desires, we will continue to suffer. When we transcend the ego we no longer have the compulsion to satisfy our desires. But how do we control the ego? It seems to have a very firm grip on us. We may even feel powerless to stop it.

## Freedom from the Ego

*We can only truly be free when we can interrupt the incessant flow of our own wants and desires and reconnect to the whole.*

To better understand what I am referring to by freedom from the ego, I will discuss the topic of death. Death of our human form, as it relates to the ego, has grown into a steady basis of fear in our modern Western culture. Death is rarely discussed. Talking about death is considered taboo for the most part and practically shunned from society. Defying death has become the purpose of most people's existence, even though everyone knows every living thing will die one day. After all, it is our natural progression.

With this mind-set, people have begun to develop habits to try to maintain the illusion they call life. People go to great lengths to preserve this sense of who they believe themselves to be. This has created an epidemic of fear. Fearful thoughts, such as guilt about our past and worrying about what is to come, have made for a life of energy-draining panic in many ways. Life is rarely lived to its fullest, because people are too focused on maintaining this perverted version of what we call life.

The ego's fear of death controls us at every turn. The only way to be free from the bondage of the ego is for the ego to die. But the ego's realization of its own impending doom is the foundation of that fear. The ego fears its own death and, therefore, works hard to be acknowledged and maintain a steady presence. The ego wants us to believe its death means the death of our true self, as well.

But there is good news. The body and mind do not have to die along with the ego. By living in the present moment, we limit the ability of the ego. Living this way consistently for a period of time reduces the ego's control over us and ultimately results in the death of the ego. When the ego no longer has control over us, we are free. This is what spiritualists refer to when they tell us to die while we're still alive, or to become an awakened dreamer, or as the bible refers to being born again. When the ego is dead, we are more alive than ever before. The death of the body has always been a constant fear of the ego, but where did this fear originate, and why do we harbor it?

## Fear of Death

*That which is born of the earth will inevitably return to the earth;*
*that which is real has always been, and can never die.*

The fear of death goes back to the very first human beings who lived on earth. We have believed ourselves to be detached from our source and allowed the egoic mind to be the supreme base of logic. Death must have been a terrifying event for those early humans witnessing it for the first time. This was when the ego cinched its claws in and tried with every effort to hold onto this futile, incomprehensible life. To this day, preserving this physical body, and keeping this life has been the sole purpose of the ego and a furtherance of the madness within our societies.

The ego thrives on fear, and fear originated from death. Before the very first death was witnessed, there was nothing to fear. Death gave birth to fear, because it appeared so final and so permanent to a mind that didn't comprehend its own divinity.

Death to the body means death to the ego. Instead of knowing death is nothing more than a transition, the ego has made death the enemy of life, a life the ego sees as tangible in the physical realm of things. In reality, life is what we are essentially, the infinite energy of Space that can never die.

Death is nothing more than the shedding of this garment that we call a body and being free of the limitations of this world. Death is not the end of anything; death is a release. As Uell S. Andersen wrote in his book *Three Magic Words* (BN Publishing 2008),

> As an organism its consciousness expands with ever-increasing rapidity, so that within a relatively short time the expanded consciousness or spirit can no longer tolerate the limitations of its form and abandons it. Thus is established the cycle of birth and death such as exists in all living organisms.

Basically, as our divine spirit, or soul, evolves in consciousness, it becomes restless. Because it is restricted by the limitations of form, it must move beyond the form, therefore relinquishing the need for the body. And the cycle repeats itself. This is why realizing our divinity is so important. The expansion of our consciousness is inevitable, and the sooner we realize this, the sooner we can make the necessary transition from a mind-dominated existence to a purposeful, divine existence.

# 7

## Relationships

*In a genuine relationship, there is an outward flow of open, alert attention toward the other person in which there is no wanting whatsoever. That alert attention is Presence.*

—*Eckhart Tolle*

In trying to understand our species, it is important to understand the way we relate to each other. Human relationships are always different, depending on whom we are interacting with. At any given time, we have various types of relationships, from parental, to spousal, employer/employee, all the way down to the stranger we pass on the street. Humans have developed a specific way of treating and interacting with people based on the roles they may play in our lives.

It is hard to have a consistently positive relationship with others, regardless of how close we are to the person or how much we may love someone. The relationship will always have good times and bad, and it will continue to be this way until we learn to allow ourselves to be detached. The word "detachment" in regard to a relationship may sound bitter or even cold, and it may appear to some as a separation or a distancing from others. This sounds contradictory to a healthy relationship. But the opposite is actually the case. Detachment, in this sense, is nothing more than allowing life to flow without resistance.

# Detachment

*Have a mind that is opened to everything, and attached to nothing.*
*—Dr. Wayne Dyer*

Detachment, in the sense I am describing, does not mean to separate or create distance from others. In fact, detachment from others will bring a more loving and caring relationship than we could have without it. Detachment simply allows others to be who they are without judgment and most important, with complete acceptance. To be detached from another person allows both people to live their own lives for their own intended purposes. It eliminates any need for things to be anything other than the way they are. Completely accepting another person, exactly the way they are, eliminates any need to be right or to cast judgment in any way.

Detachment is essential in every relationship, especially the closer the person is in relation to you, for example, parents, children, and romantic relationships. The first thing to understand is we have absolutely no control over another human being, be it our spouse, our children, our best friend, or whomever. Also, even if we do manage to manipulate someone into being who we want the person to be or having the individual sacrifice his or her desires to fulfill our needs, we will never know complete peace and happiness with the person. There will always be resentment, whether visible or buried inside.

Another thing to consider is we may never understand God's plan for anyone else. The path others are on was established long before we ever knew them, before they even took physical form.

Attachments hinder our growth as spiritual beings. An attachment is our belief a person or thing belongs to us in some way. These beliefs are some of the greatest causes of stress in our life and some of the main reasons for a failed relationship. When we are attached to a material object—our house, car, money—we can find ourselves behaving in some very emotionally (energy-) draining ways to maintain these things. We may get upset if something gets taken away, lost, or damaged. If our car is stolen, we will feel the stress and most likely anger at the fact someone took something that belongs to us. This anger or stress can turn into worry. "How will I get to work? Will the insurance company cover the whole amount of the car? If not, where will I get the money to pay it off?" These energy-draining thoughts induce a great deal of stress. This is the way we have been taught to think.

But if we know within ourselves that we are connected to Infinity, and that what we imagine to be our possessions are nothing more than things we have for a limited time, our stress and all our energy-draining emotions will subside. We will realize nothing ever belongs to us. We only have temporary control over anything at a given point in time. The possessions we have and the relationships we participate in are constantly flowing with all of life. The things we hold onto the tightest are usually the first things we will see slipping away. All we can do is appreciate the time we have been given, and make the most of it. This is detachment.

The fact our car was stolen or our house burned to the ground is a setback in what we labeled our normal life. We are taken out of our comfort zone in a sense. But putting our attention on the unlimited, overly abundant Infinity is the only way to get the things we want out of life. Spending our time frustrated or worried is sending a message to Infinity that we want more stress or more worry. None of which will get us where we want to be. All we can do is take the opportunity to find the lessons provided in any given circumstance.

Attachment, in regards to a relationship is merely our desire for someone to be the way we think he or she should be or the way we want the person to be, whether consciously or subconsciously on our part. When we love someone, we always want the best for him or her. But wanting what is best for someone and needing our idea of what is best for the individual to be the case are different things. When we are attached to someone, we become personally involved in his or her life in a way that is damaging and destined to cause suffering. Damaging when our wants and desires for him or her become conflicting or more important than the person's personal desires.

A person may want to please us by following what we think is best, or in some cases, a person feels pressured to follow what we advise at the cost of what he or she really wants. This will always bring resentment. If a person goes against what we think is best and follows his or her own path, we will be the one harnessing resentment.

By becoming detached from the person we love, however, we give the other person complete control over his or her life without any judgments. This creates liberation and peace in a relationship.

Attachment in all cases will cause suffering. This becomes especially true with the death of a loved one. It is only natural to feel pain and sorrow when someone close to us dies, but being attached to that pain can be debilitating. When we start to think someone should not have died when he or she did or how he or she did, we have attached ourselves to the death and become trapped in the egoic mind. Remember, it is not up to any of us as to when someone may pass away or even be tragically taken out of our lives. It is not an easy thing to deal with, but when we know there is a divine plan for all of it, it may be easier to handle.

As I previously mentioned, no one knows enough to question the way the universe works. Everything that happens is in divine order, even seemingly tragic events. Thinking anything should be different is our egoic mind controlling our thoughts. Thinking things should be different from how they presently are will only bring more suffering. Death is only a release from the confines of this world. Who we truly are can never die.

Accepting the fact that we do not and will never have direct control over any other person is the first step toward detachment. When there are people we care about in our lives, we can be even more grateful they are there when we are detached. It may never be possible to know when a person will leave us for any reason. Understanding this allows us to appreciate them even more during the limited time they are part of our lives. Knowing the time we have together is limited, and an end to the relationship is inevitable and unpredictable, will ultimately make us want to spend more time being happy in their presence. We look more lightheartedly on the insignificant little issues that arise.

We like to go to other people for help or advice when things go wrong in our lives. We want that reassurance or guidance from someone else in certain situations. The advice we receive may benefit us at times, but ultimately, we must follow our own divine path. Receiving guidance from others may be helpful, but it is not going to necessarily point us in the direction we need. There is a better alternative and that is to find the silent space within, and allow the infinite flow of Energy to work through us. There is no more direct or easier path to follow than the one we were placed on when we arrived here. Other people may have their opinions and advice, and some of it may be helpful in pointing us in the right direction. But we may not fully understand the motives behind anyone else's advice.

No other person on this planet, including ourselves in most cases, knows our purpose for being or the direction our path must go. Therefore, eliminate the middleperson. We should not allow anyone else's opinion about how our life should go steer us off course. We must be the determining factor in our lives. Taking advice from others may be helpful at times, but finding the direction we need to go will only ever be truly known when we allow ourselves to find our connection with God.

Now let's take a look at different types of relationships and how we can improve the way we interact with others.

## $\mathcal{P}$arent

*Teach a child to love himself above all else, and a*
*child will teach the world to love.*

Arguably the most important relationship a person can have is with a parent. The instant a child is born, he or she is dependent on another to provide the essentials of life. At that early age, a child is not capable of finding his or her own shelter and food and doesn't even have the ability to move independently from one place to another. A child needs assistance with even the basics of life. But most important, a child needs love and guidance.

One of the most common misconceptions parents have is to believe an infant or a child is inferior to them. What I mean by this is that parental figures often perceive the child to be less than they are, at least in terms of physical size and worldly knowledge. But a child is just as much a divine being as any other living thing. Actually, children often have a closer connection to their true consciousness than most adults. A child has not been subjected to the thinking mind long enough to have disconnected themselves from God, which most adults have.

It is good for parents to remember that just because a child comes into the world *through* you, it does not make him or her *yours*. A child has his or her own divine purpose, which was determined before coming out of the womb, as was the case with all of us. We were all children once. We all have our own purposes in this world, and finding that purpose is up to each of us individually.

This is not to say a child does not need guidance or that we cannot teach children the ways of the world. All I refer to is the divine purpose of a person's life, in particular of our own children. We are all born predestined to fulfill our divine purpose. This destiny is unique to us as individuals and must be realized as such.

The most important thing a parent can do to ensure the happiness and well-being of a child is to detach themselves from their children. Doing this allows the parent to accept the child exactly the way he or she was born to be. By giving all the loving attention we can to the child, knowing this child is another divine being and on a unique life path of his own, we can encourage the child to be an individual and to find his or her own path.

A child needs guidance when first learning to traverse the world. The parent's role is to guide and keep the child safe. It is obvious we should keep our children away from danger, but turning a child into the person we think he or she should be, or controlling how the child chooses to think and believe is not the role of the parent—or anyone else for that matter

My parents did not force their views onto me. Of course, they had their own beliefs about things, and I was raised to believe in what they believed in. But I was never told how to think or what I should be doing with my life. This allowed me to form my own opinions and have my own experiences. I was allowed to make the mistakes that were pivotal in moving me in the direction my life path was going. My parents loved me and did the best they could to protect and guide me, without being overbearing or smothering. I am very thankful for that. I have made more than my fair share of mistakes, and I'm sure if my parents could have, they would have done anything for me to avoid making these mistakes. But where would the lesson be in that? Mistakes are an essential part of life. No one was put onto this earth to be perfect. We all have to find our own way in life, and mistakes are often the biggest life lessons we can have.

When we show a child how to love and accept others regardless of circumstances, we make the world a better place. Notice the word "show" as opposed to "tell." We must lead by example. We cannot tell a child to love everyone and accept people the way they are when we make judgmental comments about others in front of them. We can't tell a child to have acceptance and patience, when we curse the car in front of us for driving too slowly. Starting today, make it a habit to find the lesson in each situation, and teach your child to do the same. It is amazing how transforming it can be. The amount of energy we expend on being frustrated or sending judgmental thoughts will be replaced with an increased energy from love and acceptance. This will change your life for the better and ultimately make the world a better place. The children are the future, literally, so it is incumbent on each of us to provide them the foundation they need, and to be an example for them to follow.

# $S$tranger

*When you can look into the eyes of someone who has harmed you
and see your own eyes looking back at you, then you
have come to realize who you are.*

*—Unknown*

Everyone we see on the street, share a community with, or have any type of interaction with is there for a reason. Every person on this planet has something to teach the rest of us. All the positive people we see and meet are just as important and divine as the ones who are not so positive. To an extent, how we perceive and interact with others affects the way we all think and act. There is a lesson in all interactions, and what we take from each situation depends on our interpretation of the circumstances of each event.

How can someone who is living on the street, doesn't work, doesn't pay taxes, drinks all day long, begs for a handout, and doesn't necessarily contribute to society teach us anything? The answer to this question is just as diverse as the person asking it. It isn't possible to know what this person can teach each of us specifically, but for some people, it may make them appreciate all they have. Others may see someone with a problem and want to help; that may be the lesson for them to learn.

This continuous lesson can be seen at all levels of life, and it is not always obvious. Casting judgment on someone's clothes as they walk by may be a lesson in nonjudgment when we stop to consider the reason for the judgment in the first place. Hearing a baby screaming from three rows back in the middle of a ten-hour flight may be a lesson in patience and a reminder we were all babies at one point. The fact is that nothing is random, nothing is accidental, and no one is haphazardly placed on our path in life.

I was driving home from work one afternoon, when a driver ahead of me, who was apparently not paying attention and driving much slower, suddenly veered into my lane, causing me to slam on the brakes and swerve to the shoulder of the road. Needless to say, I was not at all happy with this, since I was exhausted from work and having to deal with what I perceived as someone else's inconsideration. As the anger began to surface inside me, I caught up to the vehicle at the next stoplight and pulled beside it with my window down. The driver and passenger, a man and woman probably in their fifties, were waving their arms and looking surprised. They kept repeating in Spanish, "Disculpe! Disculpe!" I didn't even give it time to register before I shouted back, "Why don't you watch where you're going next time!" I drove off as the light turned green and, they made a left-hand turn.

As I began to drive, the anger still festering, it clicked in my head the two were asking me to forgive them. My anger immediately changed into a sort of guilt for reacting the way I did. But I immediately realized the lesson in it. We may never know what is going on inside someone else's mind, or car in this case, and we don't know what kind of day another person may be having. If we let cooler heads prevail, maybe what we interpret to be a transgression is nothing more than a simple mistake. Or maybe we happened to catch someone on a particularly bad day, which happens to us all. For all I know, the driver may have been unfamiliar with the area and just trying to figure out where he was going. It doesn't excuse the erratic driving, but we have all been in that position.

## Victim

*Nobody has the ability to affect our life unless we allow it.*

Now you're probably wondering about victims of heinous crimes or great traumatic events, and again I cannot say what is going on inside the mind of another person. What I do know is that we all have a purpose in life, and overcoming obstacles to progress and evolve our consciousness is part of that purpose. The lesson to be learned in such cases as this, however, lies with the perpetrator and the victim. I cannot tell anyone why a child was abused or why a grandmother was beaten and robbed for the twenty dollars she had in her purse. Likewise, why a caretaker would maliciously cause pain to any child or why a crook would go to such lengths to get a measly twenty dollars. We can never get behind the eyes of others and see life the way they do.

But to think anything should be different from the way it is would be to question the perfection of this life. I am not trying to downplay such events or pass criminals off as just doing "God's will." All I am saying is there is a lesson; something valuable is underneath the surface of such events, and it needs to be discovered. If you have endured such traumatic experiences, it is up to you to look within yourself and find the answers. The assistance of a counselor or a therapist may be very helpful in certain instances, but finding the peace that is within this present moment will lead to a knowing, a reconnection to the Infinite, and ultimately your liberation. This may have been the lesson all along. For all we know, the perceived wrongdoer may have been put on this planet with the sole purpose of teaching that particular lesson.

These are extreme cases, but they happen. All any of us can do is to stay present in the moment, provide assistance and comfort where we can, and take away from it the valuable lesson that is always there.

I remember a time when I was the victim of a crime. It wasn't an extreme case by any means, but the lesson was still there. I had just come home from work after traveling for a few days. It was just an ordinary day. I had been gone for a couple days, and I was looking forward to my next two days off work. As I walked to the front door of my house, like I had done hundreds of times before, I looked at the chair next to my front door and noticed it had been moved. I was living by myself at the time, and no one should have come to my house while I was gone, so I noticed something like that. But it didn't register with me until I unlocked the front door and went inside.

As I walked inside, I saw glass all over the kitchen floor and noticed all the cupboards and closet doors were open. Immediately I knew someone had broken into my house. The side door, which was made almost entirely of glass, had been shattered, and the remaining frame of the door was still partially open. I called the police and went through the house to see what was missing. The entire time this was going on, I sensed this was exactly where I was supposed to be at this moment. If this had happened a few years earlier, I probably would have been worried and upset over what had taken place, but instead, I felt a sort of calm. I wasn't happy with the situation, but somehow I was okay with it. I accepted it.

I walked around the house and saw the burglars had gone through everything. Still, I had a certain sense of peace I can't describe. I had a feeling it wasn't as bad as I could have made it out to be. A few items were taken that meant a little bit more to me than others, and I immediately accepted the fact I would never see them again. This was uncharted territory for me at the time. It was a time I could put into practice all the life lessons I had learned to that point.

As I talked to the police officer, he mentioned another burglary had happened earlier that day very close to my house, and they had caught the individuals who had committed the crime. The police confiscated items that didn't belong to the other victims. He mentioned a few of them to me, and sure enough, they were items taken from my house! Besides the broken doors, which the insurance company covered, I had almost everything back that had been stolen from me. It is not common to see a case solved and the property returned so quickly. I feel that if I had reacted differently to the situation by letting my ego take over, considered myself a victim, or believed the world was out to get me, it probably wouldn't have ended the way it did. I know I can never be a victim of anything unless I allow myself to be.

I knew the lesson that was to be learned. I knew I was meant to find the situation as it was, and it was up to me how to react to it.

I knew I could become present in the moment and connect to my divine consciousness, which I did. I wasn't upset, angry, or anything. I was at ease, because I knew the way I reacted was the way I was supposed to react; I had learned something about the way I view the world. I thought about the criminals who did this, and I didn't feel anger or resentment toward them. I actually felt sorry for them. I wondered how they had been raised or how bad their life could have been to become involved in that type of behavior. Everyone involved had a lesson to learn. I know I learned mine. I can only hope they learned theirs as well.

# Romantic Relationships

*It is impossible to truly love anything without first
loving everything about yourself.*

Almost every romantic relationship is a love-hate one. It is essential that we have control of our own life before we bring someone else into it. Bringing another person into our life to make us feel good or to comfort us is a maniacal way of relating. However, this is exactly the way most relationships work. Even scarier is the fact we think it is the way it's supposed to be. Under this idea, it is completely impossible for two people to maintain a happy relationship for long. There will always come a time when what one person does or doesn't do will cause friction.

When we are involved in this type of give and take relationship, we are operating on the level of the egoic mind. Therefore, it is vitally important to know if we want a happy relationship that works, we must begin by mastering ourselves and find out who we really are. If it is hard to be happy alone with ourselves, how can we expect anyone else to be happy alone with us? No other person or thing can bring us happiness. We already have that happiness within ourselves. We just need to realize it.

Most people look at relating to others in the wrong way. We almost always try to think, *What can these people bring to the table? What can I get from them?* When we first get to know someone in a romantic setting, we usually have the "butterflies", that excited feeling, so much so that we don't really take in all that is happening. What I mean is the normal process of getting to know someone is often skewed when we begin a romantic relationship. It's almost as if we have tunnel vision or are looking in the wrong end of a telescope.

We get so focused on what is in front of us that we fail to see the big picture. We look at another person and immediately begin to wonder, *What does this person have to offer me?* But we should turn it around and think, *What do I have to give to this relationship?* Then we can eliminate any preconceived expectations, which most people carry around with them and automatically try to interject into a relationship. Things that are so important to us that we feel we must have in a relationship. When we go into a relationship with any expectations at all, we are already establishing attachments to what that person can offer or to certain things or behaviors we expect them to possess. But if we have no expectations and only wish to give to a relationship, we are detached and able to see the person as he or she truly is. We can then determine whether this person is compatible with us. When we are complete as a person before we enter into a relationship, we don't need anyone else to fill a void, or a sense that anything is missing from our lives. This is detachment, the only way to ever begin or sustain a relationship worth keeping.

Of course, we have to be compatible with our partner. No one wants to settle in a relationship with someone who doesn't reciprocate our love. That's just common sense. When we are perfectly content with who we are, we no longer need anything from anyone else. And when we are able to enter into a relationship free from expectations, it allows more love to flourish, without the neediness or constant attention seeking that is the mainstay of many relationships.

Take a look at any online dating website, and it is quite apparent many people are lonely and feel as though they need something or someone to make them happy. Of course, there is nothing wrong with wanting to spend our time with someone special, someone we wish to make a life with. But problems arise when we think we need someone in our life to make us complete. It is paramount we learn to understand ourselves completely before we enter into a lifelong relationship. When we have predetermined expectations before we even begin a relationship, how can we possibly get the full potential out of ourselves and out of our partner? Expectations create limitations!

The romantic relationship is probably our greatest test of all. These relationships can bring us a great sense of joy, but they can also be quite insidious. The romantic relationship can be a catalyst for bringing positive energy into our lives, or it can be almost tyrannical. The reason these relationships carry so much influence is because we invest so much of who we are into them. But this attachment is the main cause for the suffering we endure. Being attached to our partner means we have a certain idea of how that person should be or how we want them to be. Essentially, we have expectations of what we want from the person and from the relationship. Having attachments will always lead to suffering and keep what could be a very special spiritual experience into misery, or at least cause bouts of pain and discomfort.

Our relationships don't have to be this way. By detaching ourselves from the relationship, we open an entirely new possibility of where the relationship can take us.

It is important to understand that by detaching ourselves from our partner we are allowing that person to be exactly the way he or she is. As Ralph Waldo Emerson said, "You love the things you love for what they are." We shouldn't love someone for what we want him or her to be. This position is very liberating. It allows two individuals to maintain their sense of being while unifying with each other. This can be the most spiritually uplifting experience there is.

No two people will ever agree on everything at every moment, but that is what makes each of us unique, and what makes each relationship a catalyst for growth when we consider the frequent variation of emotions we face. Turning a normal relationship into a spiritual practice allows each person to use the disagreements and problems of a relationship, which are bound to happen at some point, in a way that can transcend our mental judgment of the situation. Instead of choosing sides of right and wrong, we will be able to work together to find the source of the issue, which 99 percent of the time will lead back to the ego and the position of being right and making another person wrong. Once we are able to make this a habit, we will be working toward a way of removing the ego from the relationship, thus leaving nothing but divinity and a relationship built on and sustained by love.

Virtually every issue that arises in a relationship has its origin in the ego. The ego demands supremacy. When there is an argument or disagreement with a loved one, stop and ask, "What is the real problem?" By thinking another person should be acting a certain way, or that the individual is not doing what we expect him or her to do, we are judging the situation from a position of the mind. It is our opinion of how we think things should be. This is the perfect opportunity to look within and witness the emotions we may be experiencing. Watch without judgment as the emotions arise. Allow yourself to feel your body's reaction to the situation. Ask yourself if your position in the debate has its root in the egoic mind, that place of judgment and nonacceptance.

If you and your partner feel calm enough to talk and try to understand the problem together, that is mutually beneficial. But if you cannot see past the anger, jealousy, or whatever emotion has taken hold, simply allow yourself to watch the events from the position of the witness.

# 8

## Let Love Replace Fear

Emotions are essentially the body's reaction to what our mind thinks. Emotions, like thoughts, are not necessarily under our control. We don't have the ability to control which emotions we experience any more than we can control the flow of thoughts. Try making yourself feel a certain way about something, and you will see what I mean. Trying to make yourself happy when you are clearly upset is a difficult thing to do. Emotions are nothing more than thoughts, and attaching yourself to any emotion will inevitably cause suffering. We can, however, overcome any emotion by allowing ourselves to be present to it. Trying to stop an emotion from being experienced is a form of resistance and will only result in that particular emotion resurfacing until the lesson of it is learned. Not by resisting but by understanding the purpose of the emotion is the key.

Acknowledging the fact thoughts and emotions are not under our control gives us the ability to grow spiritually. When we know a particular thought or emotion is present within ourselves, we can simply allow ourselves to be in the present moment and witness the event. By allowing this witnessing to take place, we are no longer judging what is happening but allowing whatever is happening to just be. Once we become present and are able to witness the event, the emotional experience will subside, and we will be left with an understanding of why we experienced it in the first place.

Ultimately, the purpose of experiencing an emotion is to expand our consciousness.

Most of the time the emotions and thoughts we experience take root in the egoic mind. The "good" emotions are just as important as the "bad", because without one the other wouldn't be possible. The egoic mind feeds on the drama caused by negative emotions in order to maintain its existence. By causing us to associate with an emotion, we allow the ego-based mind to take control and manipulate the situation. We will never find freedom from the negative emotions if we reside inside our egoic mind. It is a constant cycle, and breaking the cycle is vital to transcending the ego. The ego feeds on drama, because when we allow ourselves to be taken in by these emotions, we give control over to our mind. Albert Einstein said, "You cannot solve a problem using the same thinking you used to create it." It is this understanding that allows us to use our thoughts to change a particular situation or event.

We can change our situation, we can change our thoughts about the situation we're in, or we can simply accept what is. Those are the only options we have. We can only evolve by allowing ourselves to be in the present moment. When we are fully present in the moment, we are accessing our connection to the divine space of Creation. This will give us the insight or momentum we need to overcome whatever the problem seems to be. Identification with any emotion has its root in the ego. Understanding the purpose of the emotion is key to the evolution of our conscious mind and a step toward realizing our divinity.

## Worry and Guilt

*To allow our life energy to be drained by anything beyond our control only furthers our suffering.*

The two most useless emotions we experience are worry and guilt. These emotions are useless, because worrying about some future event or having guilt over anything in the past is futile. It is impossible to change anything that hasn't taken place and, likewise, anything that is already over. Giving in to this way of thinking will only cause suffering, because we are taking ourselves out of the present and into our mind. We can never make anything better by worrying or feeling guilty. If the issue causing us to feel worrisome or guilty is out of our control at this moment, then being drained of energy to feel the emotion is counterproductive. Only when we accept the things we cannot change, thereby giving us the opportunity to live in this moment, will we find peace. Besides, our ego does not want us to find serenity. Worry and guilt provide just enough drama for the ego to have its presence felt.

People in relationships often use guilt when trying to get what they want from another. Parents will use it on their children; for example, a parent may use guilt when a child is graduating high school and wants to go off to college. The parent may not want the child to go too far away, so the parent will cleverly use guilt to pressure the child to stay closer to home. Guilt is also used quite often in romantic relationships. One partner may feel he or she isn't getting enough attention and may resort to guilt tactics to make the other partner feel bad about the situation. In both cases, instead of being conscious, we have allowed the ego to dominate the situation. With guilt and pressured circumstances, there will always be resentment. Maybe not at first, but it will happen. Learning to transcend the ego is necessary to maintaining a guilt-free relationship.

Worry is just as toxic. When there is a deadline or event we are dreading, we begin to worry. We take ourselves out of the present moment. Stress begins to overcome our ability to deal with the situation, and we break down physically, mentally, or both. The best way to deal with a stressful situation is to become fully present, witness the emotion, and allow our divine connection to reveal the best possible course forward. Worrying about anything beyond our immediate control is senseless.

## Jealousy and Anger

*The only way to ever get what we truly want is to live in the present moment and refuse to resist life.*

Jealousy and anger are two of the biggest fear-based emotions we can experience. Jealousy is the fear something we think belongs to us may be taken away, or that someone has what we think we should have. Anger causes us to believe we can change this moment by displaying rage. Both are nothing more than resistance.

Jealousy is an attachment, a matter of self-esteem, or insecurity over a particular matter. It is often a problem within romantic relationships, when communication is lacking. Jealousy arises when one person isn't getting the attention he or she desires from a partner or suspects the partner may be getting that attention from someone else. Jealousy in a relationship always derives from attachment. Jealousy may also be a problem in the workplace. One employee may be jealous of another, which is usually based on a certain sense of lack or inadequacy on our part. Jealousy often flares up when a person doesn't feel as adequate or resents another for being smarter or better at a certain thing.

Overcoming jealousy is all about allowing ourselves to be just the way we are. In a relationship, if we are giving all we can but not getting what we think is owed to us, problems will arise. Instead of being jealous, it's probably a better idea to examine the relationship itself. It is imperative to be completely honest with yourself when examining the relationship. Allowing ourselves to believe we are doing everything we can in a relationship, and all the blame lies on our partner may be misleading and will make it impossible to find the underlying causes of the issues.

In the workplace, accepting ourselves as we are is all we can do. If we can better ourselves, that is what we must do. If not, we have to accept the way things are and allow it to be. The older we get, the more we realize there will always be someone younger, smarter, or better looking. All we can do is accept and love ourselves for who we are. After all, if we don't love and accept ourselves, why would anyone else?

Anger is a learned emotion. As children, we may see a parent, or someone else, act out in anger and notice the anger actually resulted in the person getting his or her way about something. We may test the theory out on our own, as well. A child throws a tantrum or cries mercilessly over something wanted or for the circumstances of an event to favor him or her. And when a parent gives in to this type of behavior to calm or quiet the child, the child learns all he or she has to do is scream and shout to get what is wanted. It's the same idea in adulthood. When someone turns to anger, he or she is simply saying, "I want my way," or, "I want control."

Anger is also used as a coping mechanism in children who lack the ability to express themselves in any other way because they have never been taught any differently. As a young child, I had a bit of a temper, to say the least. I didn't like anyone touching my things, and I hated to lose at anything. I would scream, curse, kick things, and sometimes even break things. Luckily for me, however, I had older brothers. When I started to act out, I was often very quickly put back in my place. It didn't take long before I realized my actions weren't going to be tolerated, and I was able to grow out of that type of behavior.

Each circumstance will dictate how to handle someone with anger issues. This will often be by disassociating ourselves from the individual. Once they realize he or she can no longer influence us because of the angry behavior, he or she will either change approach or disassociate from us.

Of course, in cases of violence it is important to seek professional help. I am not a psychologist or a psychiatrist. I am simply trying to explain fear, the root cause of all our negative emotions. Fear is developed and harnessed within the ego. So let's take a closer look at fear.

# *Fear*

*Fear can only exist in the mind.*

Fear is the most destructive and energy-consuming emotion humans experience. All negative emotions stem from fear. Fear is what happens when we allow our ego to take control. As I explained earlier, fear is a learned emotion, but it is as ancient as history itself. We were not born fearing anything. Just look at the actions of a young child. An infant can be lying on the floor and have a large, slobbering dog standing over him or her. Though the dog is three times the child's size and has the power to cause serious harm or even death in one bite, the child will not be afraid—even if he or she has never seen a dog. Imagine yourself now with an animal you have never seen before, three times your size, standing over you. I'm pretty sure most of us would have some sort of trepidation about this.

Fear is learned through conditioning. A dog, regardless of its size, will not intimidate a child raised around dogs. But a child who may have been bitten by a dog will fear nearly every dog, no matter the size. These types of events can be observed in almost every aspect of our lives.

Our relationships have the same effect. We are not born to fear others, but over the course of our lives, we learn to label certain types of people as "bad" based on what we have been taught or what we have experienced.

Fear may stem from all types of physical and emotional pain, and eventually we begin to develop habits. We build our lives around avoiding these fears in order not to feel them again.

Not all fears need to be experienced firsthand to shape our lives. As a society, we have become fearful of many things. We are bombarded by fear on a daily basis. Just turn on a television, and you will see this. News stories are shrouded in fear. "Flu season is upon us. What will you do when you get sick?" "Mass gunman opens fire in a crowded movie theater. Are we safe anymore?" "Terrorists linked to explosion, killing ten and leaving twelve people wounded." These, and many more, are some of the headlines we hear nearly every day. We, as a species, apparently have a lot to fear. We fear becoming ill without the slightest hint of sickness in our bodies. We fear getting murdered or robbed without ever having been in a situation where this was a possibility. We fear traveling to other countries without ever having a bad experience. We fear an economic collapse that is out of our immediate control. We fear natural disasters, which, again, we cannot control, and on and on. We are being taught how to think and even what to fear, even if we don't realize it.

Some people may argue a certain sense of fear is needed to survive in the world, that it is fear of certain things that keep us from allowing harm to come our way. To that I would say there is a difference between awareness and fear. To have fear is an expectation of something unwanted to occur. Obviously, if we are walking down the sidewalk and see an angry dog barking and snarling at us, we are not going to keep walking toward it. It is not fear that keeps us from walking toward the dog; it is common sense. We do not need to be bitten to realize an angry dog may bite us.

But what are we really afraid of? Do we, as individuals, have the ability to stop any of the seemingly chaotic events from happening? No! Almost every single thing or event we fear is out of our control. We like to think that by avoiding people who are sick, staying home instead of going to the movie theater, or not traveling to any other country will protect us from the "evils" that lurk about. But when we start believing everything around us is going to cause us harm, we begin to retract from the world. We limit our existence to what we can keep at arm's reach. We shield our children from the metaphorical monsters of the world and teach them to fear these things as well. These fear-based beliefs have grown into what we have today: a society gripped by fear. Thoughts becoming things, as I discussed previously, is not subject only to material things. It is also why our fears become reality. We are manifesting what we project into the mirror of Creation and see these manifestations on a global level.

This does not mean we must roll over and allow others to cause us harm. On the contrary, if we are able to change our position in any situation, we should do so. If someone is causing us harm, it may be a lesson for us in standing up for ourselves.

This lesson of acceptance and tolerance is lacking in our world. Of course, there are people out there who will do atrocious things, like walk into a school or theater and shoot people at random. There are terrorists who would like to watch others die for their beliefs. There will always be illness in the world. The bottom line is there will always be "monsters in the closet"—if that is what we choose to think. This will always be the case until we learn to change our thoughts and learn to stop creating such madness by perpetuating the fear-based mind-set.

There may be "bad" people out there, people who are entrapped by the ego. For the sake of argument, let's say there are 7 billion people in the world, so what about the other 6.999 billion other people we share this planet with? These are people just like us, who only want to live a happy and peaceful life.

When we live in a fear-based world, we no longer see other people for who they are. We look at others as possible threats. It is easy to see the potential for disaster when we all think in this manner. This fear-based mind-set is what we are being taught and what we are teaching our children.

We all want a world that is better than the one we live in, but each of us has to do our part. Judging others and creating conflict over our own opinions of how we want things to be is maniacal. We must take responsibility for our own lives. We can never have control over another person's mind. James Allen said, "Men are anxious to improve their circumstances, but are unwilling to improve themselves; they therefore remain bound." We will all remain bound to a life of conflict and judgment as long as we remain focused on the outside world. We must turn inward, and put the focus on making our own lives better. We must stop finding fault in everyone else and make our own lives something for another generation to aspire to.

We need to reverse the fear-based mind-set that has dominated our thinking minds throughout history.

Fear has become such a normal state of being for modern-day humans that we fear virtually everything. As we discussed, these fears have emerged in physical form. President Franklin D. Roosevelt said, "The only thing we have to fear, is fear itself." This is important to know, because allowing fear-based thoughts is going to bring about the manifestation of such things. It is as simple as that. Consuming our mind with fear-based thoughts and allowing them to dictate our life is like locking ourselves inside our homes, boarding up all the windows so no one can see in, turning off all the lights, and never leaving for fear something outside could cause us pain in some form or another. Harboring such thoughts constricts our life. It is a physical and emotional drain of energy, and it takes the "life" out of life.

## Fear in History

*Let the mistakes we have made be our guide on the path forward, lest we repeat such actions again and again; and never allow the corruption of fear to dictate our destiny.*

Throughout history, fear has been quite prevalent. There are numerous examples of this, but I only need to share a few for the purpose of showing how fear can stretch the length of the planet and how we react under such circumstances.

We are all familiar with the topic of civil rights. Nearly one hundred years after the abolition of slavery, there was still very strong segregation throughout the country. Black people were sent to separate schools, forced to use separate bathrooms, and didn't earn nearly the same amount of money as their white counterparts. Women too, have experienced civil rights violations over the years. Advancements have been made, but remnants of these ideas still linger. We often fear things and people we don't understand, or those we think may be different because they pose a threat to our livelihood. A few brief examples in our modern history show just how easily fear can consume people on a large scale.

During World War II, the US government rounded up Japanese people living in the country at the time, and put them into internment camps. They may or may not have had anything to do with the impending war we faced with Japan, and many were US citizens; it didn't matter. It was a knee-jerk reaction to what the country perceived as a threat at the time. People like you and I, who did nothing wrong, were forced into these camps based on their ancestral ties. They had everything they owned taken from them. By war's end, they were sent back into society with nothing. There was no formal apology on behalf of the government until decades later, and very little was done to help them get back on their feet. However, we don't see much written about that in the history books today.

The events of September 11, 2001, set into motion some of the most imposing, fear-based legislation and action ever seen in modern US history. The Patriot Act took away the rights of anyone suspected of having ties to terrorism. There didn't have to be any evidence, and there was no due process. Wars were declared. President George W. Bush said in a speech to rally for a world coalition, "Either you're with us, or you're with the terrorists." There was no middle ground. Countries that opposed war as the first course of action were labeled weak and anti-American. Tensions rose between these nations and the United States. So-called terrorists were shipped to Guantanamo Bay, Cuba, where some were tortured and held without any date for a trial. Some had terrorist ties, while others did not.

Fear rose so quickly some people stopped thinking for themselves anymore. They gave up all thinking power to a government that may or may not have had an agenda of its own. Wars raged, and the economy plummeted. American citizens gave up many rights and freedoms in favor of what was being labeled as security. The searching of people's things without a warrant, phone taps, and surveillance monitoring of American citizens became acceptable for "the security of the nation." Creating all this fear expanded globally.

The word "terrorism," as defined by the *New Oxford American Dictionary*, means: the use of violence and intimidation in pursuit of political aims. Terrorists do not have to kill to complete their objective. The effects of the 9/11 attacks resonated long after the Twin Towers fell and continue to this day.

How much fear can we take? When will we open our eyes to the world around us and stop cowering in the corner out of fear of the unknown? Life is to be enjoyed, but this is not possible when we put ourselves in a metaphorical cage to keep out the so-called bad. The circumstances around the September 11 tragedy are mixed with controversy, and I am not trying to push any political view, I am only showing how we have come to react to fear. Meeting violence with violence is a vicious cycle that can end only when one side has completely destroyed the other. As many philosophers have alluded to, darkness cannot be cast out by bringing more darkness; only light can remove the darkness. It is this light that I speak of.

The only way to be free from fear is to allow love to prevail. I am not so naïve to think we can simply gush "honey and bunnies" into the world and our problems will simply go away. But I wholeheartedly believe when we choose to feel and express love—as opposed to hate, greed, and fear—we will make the world a better and safer place to live. Change can only take place when we each take responsibility for our own lives and remove the fear and hate that continue to fester and spread, and when we stop resisting life and learn to accept our divine paths.

I was having a conversation with a very good friend about the September 11 attacks. After I had finished saying what I have just explained here, he couldn't understand my position. The two of us have known each other for years, and our friendship goes back to our time in the military, when we were in our teens and early twenties. To paraphrase, he essentially asked me, "How can we keep our reputation as a country and maintain our strength to defend ourselves if we don't punish the ones who cause us harm? How can we allow these terrorists to attack us on our own soil, kill thousands of innocent people, and not do something about it?"

My response was that we cannot change what had already taken place, but to jump to our feet, grab our guns, and go storming into another country and kill more people is not how the world will change for the better. There were ill-intentioned people behind the attacks, and no doubt they had to be stopped. But at what cost? The cost of our freedom, or more important, at the cost of more innocent people's lives?

It is not easy to influence someone who is set on creating death and destruction, but reacting with fear and hatred toward others will produce the same results back toward us. When we have the mind-set that we need to keep building bigger and better guns to stop those who want to harm us, the ones who want to harm us will have the same reaction. This was blatantly obvious during the cold war, one of the most extreme cases of a global, fear-based mind-set, one that took us to the brink of a nuclear disaster, pushed us further into debt as a nation, and created an even greater division within the human race.

When we rid ourselves of pride, greed, and hate, we will be in a position to make change. We cannot understand how someone else thinks, but we do have the ability to change the way *we* think individually. And when we change our own thoughts, we can change our lives for the better and ultimately change the consciousness on a global scale.

## Forgiveness

*Forgiveness is the fragrance that the violet sheds on the heel that has crushed it.*

—*Mark Twain*

Forgiveness is essential to evolving our consciousness, but it is imperative to understand what forgiveness really is. Forgiveness is nothing more than our desire for a perceived wrong to be righted. It all comes down to taking responsibility for our own lives. Blaming others for our position in life is how we have come to deal with uncomfortable circumstances. It would appear to us to be the easiest way to live a satisfied life. It is important to know, however, that people are always going to act the way they know how to act. People cannot know anything they don't know, and no one can make them be any different from the way they are if they don't want to change.

Carrying unnecessary remorse, guilt, and blame (and it is all self-imposed) is like attaching a ball and chain to our ankle and trying to walk through life. It will always be there to drag us down. By accepting the fact we have made a mistake—in other words, we have done something we now know could have been handled differently—is forgiveness. Self-forgiveness is imperative. Forgiving others is only important if you blame them for something.

No one is born with the full understanding of who we truly are or where we all come from. It is our responsibility to realize for ourselves our true purpose, our divinity. It would be quite illogical to think we could do this without making mistakes along the way. If we could, we would already be where we are trying to go. There would be no point for our existence. So we must understand that no matter what we have done in our lives, or what anyone else has done in theirs, it had a divine purpose. Blaming ourselves for not doing our best or not achieving what we thought we should have for ourselves is energy draining. By accepting the fact we only acted in the way we knew how to at any particular moment is a way to advance to a higher level of consciousness. Learning from the mistakes we make is the best way to forgive ourselves.

Forgiving others, on the other hand, is only important to the extent of the blame we hold toward them. We must accept life as it is in this moment, because it is the way it is supposed to be. We must accept others as they are. We cannot control anyone else or make anyone behave in a manner that is satisfactory to our standard of living. It is out of our control.

Don't misinterpret that as meaning we should allow others to cause us harm or push us where we don't want to go. That is another story altogether. As Reinhold Niebuhr's Serenity Prayer goes, "God, grant me the serenity to accept the things I cannot change, the courage to change the things I can, and the wisdom to know the difference." Our personal opinion about how anyone else should be is simply that—our opinion. And having a mind that opposes others for the way they are is nothing but a form of resistance. This, in turn, will always lead to suffering on our account and usually into conflict with others.

We may never understand why some people act the way they do. It is not up to us to know or to judge them for it. We can only control ourselves, and in doing so will effect the rest of the world. We do not have the ability to get behind someone else's eyes and see the world the way they have been conditioned to see it.

I read a story about a boy and his teacher. The two were walking through the woods, when a pack of wolves suddenly emerged and began to pursue them. They ran as fast as they could, until they climbed to the top of a tree, losing the wolves in the process. At the top of the tree the boy asked his teacher if he was angry the wolves wanted to eat them. The teacher's response was, "Of course not. They are just wolves. They are only doing what wolves do."

That simple yet profound parable is true about every living thing in this world, especially other human beings. People are the way they are, and they can only do what they know to do. Our lives are a culmination of every experience we've ever had, so we can only know what we know right now. That goes for everyone. It is impossible to know what we don't know, and we may never know what someone else was taught or raised to understand. All the choices we ever made were made with the mind that only knew how to make that particular choice at that particular time. We didn't know anything else at the time. If we did, we may have done things differently. Of course, we can say, "I knew better than to leave the stove on that caused the fire."

But the fact it happened, regardless of what we may think we know, is a reflection of what we knew at that moment. Hindsight will always be 20/20, but learning from something we could have done differently is what the lesson is. As Søren Kierkegaard said, "Life can only be understood backwards; but it must be lived forward." The evolution of our consciousness brings us to a better understanding of what is good for us and for all of life. This is why it is generally the case that the older we get, the better we get at making good decisions.

## Acceptance

*Allow yourself to be at peace in this moment; it is always a choice.*

Acceptance means living without judgment of how we think the things around us should be. When we stop resisting the flow of life, we are accepting things the way God intended them to be. We may never know the divine plan each of us is here to fulfill. The hardships and struggles we perceive to be impediments to a happy life are nothing more than learning points. We were never promised an easy life. We were not born flawless. We are not entitled to anything.

The purpose of our lives is to transcend our ego-based minds and learn to allow our conscious connection to God to prevail, all while maintaining this human form. For this to happen, though, we must understand there will always be suffering until we learn we don't have to suffer anymore. To allow suffering is a choice each of us has at every moment. When we stop resisting, it will allow us to flow with the currents of life, instead of trying to swim against them. It means removing the judgments we have about others. To paraphrase what Dr. Wayne Dyer alluded to in, *Your Sacred Self: Making the Decision to be Free*, Judging others does not define them; it defines you as someone needing to judge others.

A common misconception regards the principle of acceptance. Acceptance is allowing life to be as it is. It is not, however, justification to allow others to cause us harm or disrespect. Acceptance may simply be that we are facing confrontation as the lesson the moment presents to us.

It is not up to us to determine the order of things. We can only deal with the circumstances at hand, using the only knowledge we have of such affairs at the moment.

## *Happiness*

*Stop seeking happiness as something that is attainable from anything tangible, and know that happiness is always present and just needs to be acknowledged.*

Happiness is not a destination. Happiness is a state of being, not a place we must strive to be in. Therefore, happiness is a choice we have in every moment of our lives, a sort of judgment call on our part. Happiness cannot be brought into our lives through any material object or even through another person. It may be hard to believe, but our happiness in the presence of that object or person is just our own subjective, mental interpretation of what we are experiencing at the time. It's a choice. We may find ourselves happier in the presence of certain people, but it is mental happiness; the human idea of happiness or love is purely mental. It is transient. The love we have for someone else can easily turn into hatred under the right circumstances, and within an instant.

True happiness or true love is an experience that goes much deeper than mere thought. It is a feeling we have inside us, a genuine knowing we and every other person are one and the same. It is a knowing all living things are one as well, and we share this collective soul.

# *Love*

*The consciousness in you and the consciousness in me, apparently two, really one, seek unity and that is love.*
—*Nisargadatta Maharaj*

There are two types of love, the human version of love and pure love. Pure love is accepting life as it comes to us, without any attachment or judgment. The human version of love is an emotion that is constantly changing. With the human version, we may love something today, and tomorrow that thing we loved may be the source of our suffering. This is often the case in romantic relationships.

Love in its purest form is a deep feeling of peace, regardless of the circumstances. Pure love occurs when we are present in the moment and life flows freely through us, regardless of whatever circumstances we may face. Pure love is always present, it cannot cast judgment, it has no expectations, it can be experienced at any moment, and it does not require another person to share it with. To have love for *every* living being equally is to know love in its purest form.

The human form of love is, at best, a dysfunctional position based in our human mind. This version of love is often short lived and is usually spent with short bursts of seemingly euphoric feelings, which most assuredly will not last. Then come the feelings of disinterest, loathing, bitterness, jealousy, and even hatred. There can never be lasting love in the human version, because the ego simply won't allow it.

Pure love, on the other hand, is something that originates in the vastness of infinity. There is no opposite or contradiction to this type of love. True love is complete acceptance. It has no beginning and no end. The love one can feel for God—or more accurately stated, the love God has for us—is as close as I can come to describing it in words. Accepting and allowing others to be who they are is pure love. Pure love is complete acceptance without expectation or limitation.

# Part 3

# The Path

# 9

## The Journey

Today you will travel to earth. It is a planet that has various forms of beings, and it will require you to adapt to an environment. The rules are more constricting there, and you will be given a mind with the ability to think on its own. This mind will be a very powerful tool in making your way through the so-called life you will live, but this mind will also be your biggest adversary. You will be given a body that will be able to experience sensations you are not familiar with.

Earth will allow you to experience life in a way that is not possible here. You will be able to feel physical feelings and emotions, and to see physical beauty. The body you will have will be your home. Be careful that you don't allow your mind to trick you into thinking your body or your mind is who you actually are.

You will be surrounded by other beings with bodies of their own. They, too, will have a mind to think with and will often think differently from you. But don't forget the other living beings you see are just costumes covering the divine nature you all truly are. Never forget that regardless of how different any other being may appear to be, you are all one, and you always have a connection to me.

This experience will be challenging, but it will also be very pleasurable and glorious if you choose to make it so. Always remember that who you truly are is divine, and you should be able to navigate the world with ease. You have a specific goal to accomplish while you are in physical form, but if you just allow life to guide you and don't resist the course you are to take, you will be just fine. Enjoy!

The illustration I just described is a fictitious conversation God may have had with us before we arrived here on earth. We have all come from the divine Space that surrounds. In part 3 I describe the path our lives take from before we come to this planet to where we return to our Source. I explain this journey as a path we are all on and will continue to follow while we accomplish the objective of this life. The purpose of our being may not be obvious to us, but the fact that we are here and being guided along this path is the most important thing to understand.

This chapter is a culmination of all the topics I have discussed so far. My intentions are to describe the ideas of this book in a way that we can all relate to, starting with our existence before we took human form.

## Coming to Life

*We are in this world, but we are not of this world.*
—*Unknown*

Who or what we fundamentally are is the "soul," or the conscious mind we perceive to reside within this body. The soul is the divine space that is now and has always been the makeup of Infinity. The importance of the soul taking shape inside this body, and the acquisition of the senses we experience, is vital to completing the objectives of our existence. It affords us the opportunity to experience life with sensations and thoughts, which are not possible in the true realm of our existence.

The mind has been designed to operate on a physical level. It is up to each of us to realize, at some point in our existence, that this mind is not what we are. Our purpose is to discover we are part of the divine makeup of infinity and allow that knowledge to guide us through this physical world.

Before our birth into human form, we were still the all-encompassing divine Space. We each knew the fundamental objective we were born to carry out before taking human form. But once we took this physical shape, we were given this human mind and allowed to think. Having this mind gives us the ability to think independently from God, or Infinity, and allows us to see exactly where we came from. The body we have is unique in that we have never known such limitations. We are naturally a free spirit, so to speak.

Soon after birth, we begin to use the human mind to understand this new place, but before long, this mind will consume the way we see and think. We will disconnect from the source of our Creation and think only in worldly terms. We no longer know ourselves as divine beings. We now see only physical form and an ever-changing physical world.

## The Journey Begins

*The path of life varies for each of us, but they all merge in the end.*

Imagine walking down a path. It can be anywhere: a nature trail in the forest, a boardwalk at the beach, or even a worn-down path through a meadow. Now imagine this path is only accessible and visible to you, and you have always been on the path since the day you came out of the womb. This path is your entire life, including your body in physical form. The scenery and the environmental conditions are constantly changing, but we know we have an objective to complete, so we press on. Sometimes the path is clear-cut and easy to follow. Other times, we lose the trail and have to find our way back on course. We are always moving forward, regardless of whether we want to or not.

The time we have in this body is limited. Therefore, it is imperative for us to realize that following the path God has laid out for us is the easiest way to make it in this life. This path is not our design but God's, and resisting the course we are to take will only cause us to suffer.

The journey begins when we first emerge from our mother's womb; we are already on the path set up for us. Some of us were born onto a path of ease and comfort from the beginning. Others were born into chaos or suffering almost immediately. This was not something we had any control over. This is the purpose of our lives. The circumstances under which we came into the world are not up to us to dictate.

We have a choice, though it may not be clearly known at the time. We can choose to press forward on this path, or we can start to resist what we have been given. It may never be clear why we were born into specific circumstances, but it is not for us to decide.

People who care for us may surround us, or we may have no one there who cares for us when we first arrive. Nonetheless, the path keeps moving forward. Change is continuous, and we are not able to stop it. We have the choice in every moment to accept what is given to us, to change the circumstances we have, or to resist it all and allow suffering.

We have little control over things during our first couple years of life. We rely on others to provide for us all we need to survive. If we are lucky, we will have caregivers who provide us with sustenance and give us love. If we are not so lucky, we may endure severe hardships. Again, it is not up to us to decide whether what we have been given is fair or unfair. The situation we were born into and which we must endure was the course we were given. It is up to us to learn the lessons provided along the path of life.

Contrary to popular belief, we are not born equal, in worldly terms. We do not share the same advantages, nor do we all share the same disadvantages. We are not all here with the same lessons to learn. We each have our own course to follow, but we can all move toward the same end. We are never able to choose the places we arrive or the families we have when we are born. The purpose for each of these factors is part of the details of our life path.

The world may seems unfair when some children are born into wealth and privilege, while others are born into pain and suffering. But resisting the things we cannot change will cause greater suffering. Besides, our divine purpose is intricately interwoven into all aspects of our lives.

As we progress through life, we interact with many people. Some of them become great guides for us on the path of life. Others only seem to cause us pain. But everyone has a part to play in this story we call life. Each of the people we interact with has a lesson to teach us and is just as divine as any other person we meet on our path.

There are times in life when we will get frustrated with the way we are living and may look to other people for direction. A key thing to remember is that no one can access our life path unless we allow it. Similarly, no one is to blame for the circumstances of our lives. It is our path to follow; no one can live this life for us or tell us how to live it for ourselves unless we give permission.

We may have family members, friends, teachers, or counselors who can give us life-changing advice and point us in the right direction. There may be people who cause us pain, either emotionally, physically, or both. But none of them can get into our souls. The soul is where our true self resides, and no physical being can access this part of who we are.

No one knows where our path will lead, and no one can see it but us. We may be swayed, or even forced, by others to try to choose a different path, but we are the only ones who know where our paths lead. Some people may try to push us in another direction, and may well have good intentions; others may try to do so for selfish reasons. Regardless, it is always up to us to decide the course our lives will take. It may take courage at times, and it will definitely take faith, but to fulfill our divine purpose and experience the reason we were put here to begin with, we must follow our heart, which will always lead us in the right direction.

We must set aside any feelings of guilt in deciding to live our own lives. To live the life we choose is not being selfish; it is being courageous. Some people aren't happy with the paths they are on and may want to live vicariously through us. But giving in to their demands and wishes will always leave feelings of emptiness inside of us. This is your life, no one else's.

# Obstacles

*We are entitled to nothing. Life is what we choose to make of it.*

We are not born into this physical world as perfect beings. The source of infinite Space that we are fundamentally is a perfect being, but in this body, we do not see that perfection until it is realized. The lives we lead are filled with choices and feelings of good and bad. We progress through learning the ways of the world and by growing and expanding our consciousness.

As we walk along the path of life, we experience days that are sunny and beautiful, but we also experience days that are cold and rainy. The path may be easy some days, but others may be filled with challenges. The challenges we face may be as simple as crossing a stream in one instance or as great as crossing a raging river in another. This is equivalent to dealing with the day-to-day tasks we face. From having a bad day at work to dealing with tragedy or loss, it is up to each of us to find our way over the obstacle. Some of the obstacles are easy to overcome, while others may be quite taxing and require us to fail again and again, until we realize how to navigate them.

# Resistance

*Resistance to life is the belief we think we know more than God.*

We have a choice to make each time we encounter obstacles on our path. We can deal with the situation at hand, or we can give up and try to find our own way around them. When we resist what is, we are ultimately fighting against life itself. By dealing with the situations as they arise, we will experience varying degrees of discomfort (suffering). But after we have hurdled the issue, we have learned the lesson we were meant to discover. When we decide to try to navigate our own way around a difficult issue, we take ourselves off of the path. We essentially tell God his way of progressing is not working for us, and we then try to make our own way in life. This may seem like the easiest way of dealing with things at the time, but it takes us off course, and we are left wondering where we went wrong. We will inevitably be faced with a similar dilemma in the future. The problem will not go away, until we realize why the problem exists in the first place. It may be masked, and it may show up in a different shape in the future, but it will keep returning until we have learned from it.

Extreme examples of this may be abusive or codependent relationships and drug and alcohol abuse. Most people who have endured these types of events often repeat the cycle throughout most of their lives, without ever realizing why.

When people are born into situations that don't provide them with good foundations for life, they often grow into adults who do not know how to cope with circumstances they must face. Turning to substances to mask the pain may seem like the easiest way to remain in this world. Temporarily covering the pain they face with drugs or alcohol can only dull the pain for so long, before the wounds are opened up again. And each time, the pain gets harder to deal with. Addicts crave more and more of the substance and will often go to great lengths to get what they need to make the pain go away, even for a moment.

This all goes back to the ego. As I talked about in a previous chapter, the ego causes us to crave anything it can to keep itself alive. People this far into addiction or similar circumstances are so lost in the egoic mind that they cannot see past it. They are too far from seeing their own divinity. Their world is limited to the control their egos have over them. They forget the beauty that is within them and about their divine connection. In the most extreme cases, a person is drawn to suicide as the only escape he or she can conceive of to find release from the hold of the ego. We all need to understand the ego, and we all need to realize we can take back control.

This is not just the case for people with severe addictions but also for most all of us who experience pain and suffering as obstacles of our lives. The case of the addict is just an extreme case. People who face financial difficulty, parents who have problems with a child, and people who dislike the job they have and feel stuck are all cases of people facing obstacles on the path of life. Anything that takes us out of the present moment is an obstacle to the evolution of our consciousness. We can learn to view these situations as objectives to overcome instead of problems with no solution. When we realize the obstacles were put there intentionally for us to navigate, we can accept the circumstances and either deal with or change them.

When we look at adversity in this light, we can become better and better at noticing problems as they arise. We will then be able to see an obstacle in the distance and learn to handle the situation before it even becomes a problem for us. Staying stuck in a situation we don't want to be in is a choice we make. We must stop making excuses for our lives and create the changes we want for ourselves. No one is going to make this life better for us. It is up to each of us to find our way.

# Crossing Paths

*Our life is our own, and no else has the power to
influence us, unless we allow it.*

The people we encounter on a daily basis are crossing our path
during that instant. They each have a path of their own, but for that
specific moment in time, the two paths intersect. Some people cross
and are gone within a moment. Others cross our path and remain
there for years, or even a lifetime. We do not always choose whose
paths we cross, but we always have a choice with whom we will share
our path. We have a choice at any time to remove ourselves from
that shared path, even though it may not always be easy. We each
have the ability to attract into our lives those people who are going
to love us for the person we are.

From the time we come into this world, we are on our own
path. Our parents, the nurse, the doctor, and everyone else in
the room is only sharing our path at that particular moment.
For most, our parents or caregivers will remain on our path for
several years, if that is what we choose to allow. Parents often
forget their children are separate, divine beings and try to control
the direction and the path their children will go. In a romantic
relationship or a marriage, people forget that uniting as a couple
does not take away from the fact there are still two paths being
followed; however, we have allowed someone else's path to parallel
our own for a time.

It is also important to remember no one can determine the
extent or amount of time anyone may share in the course of our lives.
When we allow someone else to remain on our path, we do not have
the ability to know how long that person may stay. And the course
of another person's path is never known to us.

## *Lessons Learned*

*Life is simply about the joy of living, and everything that happens along this journey is divine.*

It is no accident that we know more about life in our last days than we did when we first arrived. We experience different things in life to teach us what we need to learn, but not everyone is here to learn the same things. Buddhism talks about reincarnation, and the Buddha believed he had been many different forms, including plants, insects, animals, and even other human beings. One cannot be certain if this is true, but it is one way of looking at life.

Whether we are going to keep repeating life or are here only once, there are plenty of lessons we can learn. Every action has an equal and opposite reaction, as Sir Isaac Newton's law of motion states, and every action we make effects every other life form on the planet. Similarly, everyone else's actions affect us; it's the butterfly effect theory.

Some people may actually be on this earth with the sole purpose of teaching us a lesson. Maybe that person we pass on the street, or the person who vandalized our car, or the person who paid us a compliment that brightened our day is actually God in human form. As Mother Theresa called her work, "Helping Jesus in all his distressing disguises." God is everyone we pass on the street or have any interaction with. Though the body that carries each of us may be different, what we are inside is all the same. We are all infinite souls, a drop of water in the ocean of life but all water, nonetheless.

## Fading Away

*The body is a cloak, a garment that will be shed when
we are called back home.*

We are brought into this life for a purpose. That much we know.
But what happens when we have completed our tasks in the physical
form and it is time to return to Infinity? It has been said the only
certainty in life is death. No one has lived in physical form forever.
We will all one day cease to be. When it comes time to shed this
garment we call a body, we will give our bodies back to the earth,
and our true essence, our divine spirit, will remain, just as it has
always been, a part of the infinite Energy.

This path of life is often windy, sometimes dark, but always
necessary. As we grow in consciousness, it can be a beautifully fulfilling
journey. We have a choice with every step we take how we want to
proceed. Do we continue to walk down the path, navigating every
obstacle and enduring even the most painful and uncomfortable
experiences, knowing even the hardships are purposeful and beauty
abounds? Or do we give up and try to make it on our own? To go down
the path is to allow life to be as it is. But to go off course is to resist this
life. In resisting, we tell God we know better than he does about how
to live life. To resist this life will cause unnecessary suffering.

This very moment is the time of our lives. Not yesterday, not
tomorrow, not even five minutes from now, but this very moment!
There is nothing we can do to change the past and nothing we can do to
ensure our future. The only time we will ever have is now. We can never
connect to God through the human mind. We must learn to quiet our
minds and allow ourselves to reconnect to our infinite energy Source.
When the mind stops operating, we are driven by our conscious minds
and directly connected to Infinity. At that point, anything is possible.
When we are connected to God, we are able to make change not only
in our own lives but in the world, as well. It is through this change that
we will have a positive impact on the entirety of existence.

# Part 4

# Moving Forward

# 10

## Change

In realizing our divinity, we are capable of changing the world in unimaginable ways. The past is the past and will always be so. The future is never certain. Living in the present moment and taking responsibility for our own lives is the only way of advancing toward a peaceful, joyful world. The seemingly chaotic events we see every day are only purposeful until we realize life doesn't have to be so hard, and suffering of any kind is only the result of our thoughts. Stepping out of the ego-based mind and allowing our divine consciousness to expand are essential in creating the change we need to move forward.

Each of us arrived in this world as an imperfect being, albeit with a perfect consciousness, which most people still do not realize. We have a great tool in the functioning human mind to aid us in living in this physical realm. But we mistakenly identify with the mind and believe it to be our true self.

Since we were born with a seeming imperfection and the course of this life is constantly changing, there are many areas in which we may desire to see changes made. These areas may include all our existence, from our physical bodies, our material possessions, and even our spiritual presence. We probably want healthier, more physically fit bodies. We want nice houses to live in and nice cars to drive. And I think that if you are reading this, you probably want a sense of purpose and a better understanding of the spiritual aspect of your life, or at least a knowing of whom you truly are. As human beings, we are also able to connect to our infinite Source and become more present spiritual beings.

The first and most important step in bettering your life situation is to conduct a self-evaluation. I mean really become curious about whom we are as people and whom we truly are as divine Beings. Question the most fundamental understandings you hold to be true for yourself, such as Does my body really exist? Am I part of the infinite universe of Energy? Where did I come from, and where will I go when I leave this body? As you begin this inquiry, you will probably have hundreds more questions like this.

From there you can start to evaluate the current physical condition of your body. Are you happy with your body? Are you eating a healthy diet? Are you getting enough sleep? Do you get enough exercise?

Take it even further, and extend your self-examination to the world around you. Are you happy with your personal relationships with your loved ones? If not, what is lacking? What can *you* do to change it? Are you happy with your day-to-day life—work, school, or whatever else may occupy your time?

This type of questioning can go on and on, all the way down to the most miniscule details of your life; there really is no end. But first and foremost, you must be completely honest with yourself. The spiritual aspect of your life will reveal itself to you as long as you keep an open mind and a willingness to explore that avenue. Your personal life, however, needs a much more honest and direct focus of attention. It will be counterproductive to want to have something change while you are not being honest with yourself.

## *Our Bodies*

We are constantly bombarded by celebrities and models. We can't turn on the television or computer without seeing society's depiction of beauty: thin, perfectly sculpted, a bright white smile. Everywhere we look are billboards and signs advertising something endorsed by some "beautiful" person. Now there is nothing wrong with wanting to be attractive or physically fit, but I believe we, as a society, are getting far too carried away with the interpretation of beauty. Popular culture has influenced us to the point where we no longer accept the way we have been made, and insists on needing a specific body type or image in order to fit in. It has become so easy for us to find flaws in someone who may be different in size or have some physical characteristic that is different from what most people consider attractive. We look at ourselves and also find flaws.

It is very important to understand no one chose his or her body at birth. We did not get to go shopping for a body before we came to live on this planet. We can't help having the body type we have. We had nothing to do with the fact we come from a genetically large family, that our skin is a certain color, or our nose is too big for our face. We had no control over any of it when we were born. Of course, we all have certain physical characteristics we would like to change. We want to be taller or shorter, have more hair or less hair, more muscle, bigger breasts; the list goes on.

It has become nearly impossible for each of us to accept ourselves the way we are, and creating society's version of a desirable self-image has become a relentless task for many people. But the idea of desiring society's version of beauty is nothing more than our ego trying to find an identity.

Because we were born a certain way does not give us permission to feel sorry for ourselves or blame others for our lot in life. In today's day and age, it is possible to have an operation or take some drugs that will give us the physical appearance we desire. But ultimately, we must accept ourselves for who we are. As I have already discussed, the ego will not stop craving more, and that is exactly why we feel the need to change in the first place.

Being overweight or out of shape is a personal choice for most, unless there is a medical condition or other such factors to consider. Our body frames are generally attributed to genetics, but allowing ourselves to live an unhealthy lifestyle and be out of shape is a personal decision. It is not our genetic makeup that has us drinking soda and eating junk food every day. And it is not our genetic makeup that causes us to take the elevator instead of the stairs. "Well, its diet soda, and I would rather ride the moving walkway than walk the fifty feet to the exit," is what I often hear. This goes back to what I mean about being honest. If we want to really see a change in our bodies, we have to be brutally honest with ourselves. Then we need to change the thoughts that got us into this position in the first place.

I was walking through the airport the other day when I noticed a man on crutches. He had one leg amputated above the knee. Instead of having a prosthetic or sitting in a wheelchair, he was on crutches and moving rather quickly, pulling his rolling bag behind him with one of his hands. I was amazed at watching this man. This guy didn't quit and say, "Well I know my place in life." He didn't sit around feeling sorry for himself. I was inspired! The next airport I arrived at had only one escalator, which was out of service, and passengers were forced to use the stairs. I've rarely seen such outrage at something so insignificant. The people, who had all their appendages, complained about taking the stairs. I just thought of the man on crutches. I'm sure he wouldn't have minded taking the stairs if he were able. It just goes to show how, as a society, we have become so reliant on the little luxurious most of us take for granted every day.

Becoming physically fit and maintaining that lifestyle are not as difficult as we have made ourselves believe. We lead busy lives, with kids, work, and school, and we don't have time to go to the gym or put on the running shoes every day. But it's all a matter of priority. We have time to watch a few hours of television each day or surf the Internet, do we not? This was the question I posed to a friend who insisted there was no time in the day to get the exercise he wanted. "I don't have the energy to spend my entire day working, only to come home, exhausted, and force myself to exercise," he said. I replied, "You would probably have more energy if you exercised more often."

We don't always have time to work out, but we do all have a choice about whether we are going to walk a little further from the parking lot or take the stairs instead of the elevator or escalator. And we all have the choice to drink water instead of soda or have a salad instead of a cheeseburger. If we incorporate little things like this into our day, our mind-set will change, and we will begin to make real changes in our health.

## Our Relationships

The same honest approach can be made in our personal relationships. Take a plastic bottle, without a cap, and squeeze it in your hand as tightly as you can. Then hold the squeezed bottle underwater, without releasing the grip, and see how much water it will retain. Now loosen your grip on the bottle, and let the water fill the bottle to its maximum capacity. This illustrates many relationships we have. We hold on so tightly lest someone should leave us. We convince ourselves that if we just hold on a little tighter, we can control another person's fate, as it pertains to being a part of our lives. Having attachments to other people is a surefire way of creating unnecessary stress in our lives. Smothering people under the weight of our desire to retain the relationship is always going to have a bad result. Loosening our grip on the people we love allows that love to flourish without the heavy weight of attachment.

Another area we need to consider is how we listen in relation to others.

# Listen

The question you should ask yourself the next time you are having a conversation is, Am I listening to what the other person is actually saying, or am I just waiting to speak? Much of the time the latter is the case. We are all guilty of doing this from time to time. Or worse, we interrupt someone or wait until he or she is finished only to share a similar, yet slightly better, story compared to the one the person just shared with us. This is known as the "one-up." I have been talking about something and notice the other person isn't even looking at me or acknowledging me. It doesn't take long for me to end a conversation like this. Of course, I have been on the opposite end of that type of conversation as well. I have made a conscious effort to change that habit, and I have realized the amazing amount of information I have learned as a result.

Everyone wants to tell his or her story; it is a side effect of the ego. Try listening in any type of relationship, and you will be astounded at how effective and transformative it can be. Listen when your spouse is complaining about his or her day and when a coworker wants to rant about something or tell a story. Try to listen without adding your experiences to the conversation. Try it for a week, and it will soon become very obvious that the ego is always present when you feel the need to talk about yourself. You don't need to justify your life experiences or impress anyone with the stories you have. You know where you have been and what you have accomplished.

I have been guilty of this in my life. I used to feel the need to impress others or establish myself with the accomplishments I had. But in doing so, I could see how it affected the way people looked at me. No one wants to hear gloating or a self-centered response when he or she is the one talking. Feeling the need to constantly boast or brag is a sign the ego is present. Holding onto the past and trying to maintain images of who we were is the work of the ego. This way of thinking is self-destructive. Listening to others is an easy way to begin strengthening any relationship and is very important in changing your life for the better.

## Love Yourself First

As I discussed earlier, the only way we can love anything is to completely love ourselves first. This is probably the single most significant way to live a happy, purposeful life. The idea of loving ourselves first may sound conceited or selfish, but love for the self is paramount. Having great love for ourselves sets a standard for how we allow others to see and treat us. It is easy to see when we look at someone who may have little self-respect or low self-esteem. They are treated according to the way they teach others to treat them, and that is based on how we treat ourselves. We cannot command respect from anyone if we don't already have it for ourselves.

When loving ourselves is the predominant type of love we have, we are able to express that love out into the world. We will begin to become what we continuously think about, or as Earnest Holmes said, in *Creative Mind* (Wilder Publications 2010), "It is not enough to say that we attract what we think; we become what we think, and what we become we will attract." If all we have inside is self-loathing or a diminished image of ourselves, that is what we become and what we attract into our lives. This is quite visible in our personal relationships to other people. It has often been said that we judge a person by the company he or she keeps. Like attracts like, and vice versa.

Far from being selfish, loving yourself first is the most beneficial advice we can use in making ourselves into the person we wish to be. Loving ourselves first begins with being completely honest with ourselves, sometimes even brutally honest, to see past the false sense of self we have built up over the course of our lifetime.

# Be Honest

Being internally honest is pivotal in creating change within our own lives. Honesty is often overlooked when we decide to make any sort of personal change. It is easy to get hung up on the past as it relates to moving forward. It is easy to put blame on others for the circumstances of our own situations. "My parents never loved me," "My father was never there for me," "I was bullied as a child," and on and on. I am not downplaying these specific life situations or any such events of anyone else's life. I am only trying to draw attention to the fact that we all have had something or someone in our lives that affected the way we view things.

In being honest with ourselves, at this very moment, how can actions that happened in the past affect the decisions we make today? The only way anyone can affect us in any way is if we allow him or her to do so, and it is a conscious effort on our part to do it. We cannot change the past anymore than we can foresee the future, but what we do have is this moment right now! We each have the ability to make a choice about whether we want to continue allowing the past to dictate how we live our lives. Making the choice to disassociate from the past may take a tremendous amount of courage, but if you are serious about making real, long-lasting change, it is not only necessary but essential.

As I mentioned earlier, we didn't get to pick the circumstances into which we were born, but we all have, in this moment, the opportunity to make this life the one we want from here on out. And if there are people surrounding us who will not allow us to see our full potential, evaluating the company we keep may be a good place to begin a revision. We are each responsible for the circumstances of our lives, regardless of how we feel about it.

There is no one to blame for our own particular life situation. We are the only one with the power to make our own life better or worse. Everything else is only a judgment or choice on our part. Understanding that everything and every situation is necessary for the evolvement of our consciousness, and that we are all on this path for a purpose, should make life easier. Regardless of how we feel a certain person should act or how a particular event should have played out is irrelevant; it happened, nonetheless. The only true way of moving past this point in our lives is to accept what has taken place and learn from it.

# 11

## *Growing Spiritually*

What is the most restricting circumstance we as a species face in moving forward in the world today? What is the most predominant problem keeping us from having a peaceful existence? These are the questions I used to ponder every time I looked at a newspaper or turned on the television. The current state of the world is a chaotic one at best, at least from the perspective of the violence and greed we are exposed to every day. I used to believe fear was the single most significant issue that plagued humankind, creating the problems we have in the world today.

Fear, as I have discussed at various lengths throughout this book, can cause people to react to the world in an outrageous fashion, but the further I explored the topic, the more I realized that what the Buddha taught is very true: "All of life is suffering, and we will continue to suffer until we realize that we don't have to suffer anymore." I wanted to share this quote again, because it bears repeating. Fear is a part of the problem, but it is not the root. Fear is only a side effect of the underlying cause, and that cause is our own human mind, the ego. And suffering is a result of the desires of that ego.

Today, the transcendence of our consciousness is becoming more visible. By consciousness, I mean the inner being or infinite Energy. I see a country—a world—evolving to a point unprecedented in the human species' time on this planet. Divisiveness has been a constant and has gradually grown stronger over centuries with war and hatred. But a movement beyond this division of the human spirit is showing its face. Scenes of heroism are seen in every tragic event we endure, from terror attacks to natural disasters. The human spirit always emerges in the face of atrocity. We are much stronger and more interconnected than most people realize.

In our modern society, narrow-mindedness and lack of tolerance are being peeled back. It's been a long time coming, and there's obviously still a long way to go. But I believe in our lifetime we will see love and acceptance reach heights beyond anything most people today would have ever guessed possible. Within the last century alone, we have seen tolerance advance further than in the previous few centuries combined. It is with the change in a global consciousness that this is possible.

There is an idea, a knowing that things can change. Things today can be better, and the world can advance. We just have to learn to use our minds for the purpose it was intended and to live in the present moment. It all starts with a thought. When enough people begin to ask the right questions and begin looking inward for the answers, global consciousness will evolve. We will begin to experience life the way it was meant to be experienced. When we learn to go beyond the mind, we will all see a transformation unprecedented in any previous generation.

## Beyond the Mind

What is enlightenment, and why is it so important? Why should we want to live an awakened life? What benefit could it possibly bring? These are the types of questions people often ask. It is essential to understanding our existence and will ultimately determine the fate of our world.

We live in a world where communication and information come fast and are seemingly unending. We are constantly seeking some form of mental stimulation. The human mind does not relent. We don't give ourselves a break from the noise. We simply do not allow ourselves that luxury. Most people are very uncomfortable in silence. Stopping the outer chatter of the world is as troublesome to most as trying to stop the inner chatter we experience. Just try driving back and forth to work one day, and leave the radio off. Put the cell phone down, and allow the silence to be present. If you are not used to being in silence, you may feel a certain discomfort. The discomfort is nothing more than the ego becoming restless and desiring to be noticed. When the mind is not constantly occupied, it actually has a chance to slow down or even stop. This is terrifying to the ego, because a silent, still mind is a mind living in the present moment, a place where the ego does not exist.

We seem constantly connected to some sort of electronic device. It is very obvious when we are sitting anywhere and constantly doing something on our cell phones. When we are at home, the television or computer seems to always be on. At night, lying in bed, more television. As the seventeenth century philosopher, Blaise Pascal said, "All of mankind's problems stem from his inability to sit quietly in a room alone." This is a reference to allowing the silence, or the reconnection to our divine presence, to quiet the mind's endless conversation with itself. By affording ourselves the opportunity to quit talking and quit thinking, we allow ourselves the opportunity to reenergize and refresh our body, mind, and spirit. We are reconnected to Infinity.

When we learn to separate our true selves from our minds, we can experience the most euphoric sense of peace. All the trivial things of the world seem to fade away, and we can experience pure joy and oneness. As I explained at the beginning of this book, silence is the one true language that God speaks. All people from every corner of the planet know and understand this language. Do nothing but allow yourself the opportunity to reconnect and to shut down your mind each day, and the results will be astonishing.

# *Reconnect*

When trying to allow silence, it is counterintuitive to just turn off the television or computer and sit alone with nothing more than our thoughts. Doing this will exacerbate the problem, because what you are doing is allowing your human mind, your ego, to wander. What I recommend is any form of meditation. This may be a scary word to some people, because most people who have never undertaken any form of meditation believe it takes a lot of hard work. Meditation, in the sense of quieting the mind, can be as simple as focusing on each breath or simply watching the thoughts as they flow through the mind. It is nothing more than being present in the moment.

If you are not familiar with meditation, I recommend it as something to look into. Meditation does not necessarily mean sitting cross-legged for hours, with your thumb and middle finger touching. It can be anything from counting your breaths to repeating a mantra.

However, even without meditation, there are many ways to slow your thoughts and allow yourself to reconnect to God, the place where all answers and all of the peace of Infinity can be found. Find what works best for you.

The objective is to stop identifying with any thought and even silence the inner voice, which will allow pure consciousness to preside over us. If you have never done anything like this before, I recommend breath counting in the beginning. Breath counting is exactly what it sounds like. Lawrence LeShan, In *How to Meditate* (Back Bay Books 1974), describes several methods of meditation, in particular, breathe counting. Count each inhalation and exhalation as one; do this up to a count of four and repeat the process. With each breath, all your focus should be on the air coming in and the air going out. Feel the air as it enters the nostrils and fills the lungs. Notice, too, the air as it passes over the lips and as all the tension in your body is released with each exhalation.

To think of this as meditation may be a foreign idea to some, but it is something we have always been taught to do. When we are angry or upset, we are often told to take a deep breath, there is a purpose behind this.

Another easy way to become present in the moment is to watch the thoughts as they flow through your mind. This is one of the easiest ways I have found to reconnect, because stopping the thought altogether is almost impossible for me at times. Basically, what I do is find a quiet place to sit. I focus on my breathing until the thoughts begin to surface. As they do, I simply watch them. I do not allow myself to identify with any particular thought; that is key. I just watch the thoughts as if there were a movie projector in my head. The mind's identification with anything is the ego's way of injecting itself into your life.

When you are looking for an answer to a particular problem, you must go inside yourself. Shut down the mind, and allow the silence to take control. This silence is the infinite energy working through us; it is our connection to our true being. It is profound to realize when we stop the incessant flow of thoughts, we are able to center ourselves and become serene. This is our reconnection with God.

Any type of physical exercise is great when it comes to slowing our thoughts. Yoga, in particular, is a great way to bring the body, mind, and spirit into balance, but any form of exercise can work. Bringing attention to the exercise itself and focusing on each muscle as it contracts and relaxes is all that is required. The key word is "focusing." This concentration is beneficial in two ways: (1) it allows us to practice good form and technique in each repetition, which will increase strength and reduce our susceptibility to injury, and (2) it focuses the mind on the matter at hand, which brings us into the present moment.

Running is one of my favorite hobbies, because I get to be outside, and it is very liberating. But each person has his or her own likes and dislikes. The main thing to remember is to find something enjoyable. If you feel like you have to force yourself to exercise, you will not stay with any exercise program very long, and your results will reflect your disinterest.

Going into nature is probably the easiest way to reconnect. It is natural for us to feel at peace in nature, because we are away from the busy, mind-numbing world of thought, and everything in nature constantly resides in the present moment. Being in nature allows us to connect with life without the mental distractions. In nature we can feel the presence of all the other living things around us. The sheer beauty and awe of nature can bring us to the present moment in an instant. Admiration for the natural beauty we find in the outdoors is an appreciation for the beautiful lives we have been given.

Any activity that allows us the opportunity to become completely involved is beneficial. Any type of art project, home construction, working on or cleaning our car, yard work or gardening are all things we routinely do already. The main thing to remember is to focus on being in the moment, simply being aware of the activity we are presently involved in, even if, or especially if it is not something particularly enjoyable or interesting. Most people say they love to exercise, because it gives them a chance to clear their mind, or to garden, because it is relaxing. This is the place I am referring to. Just be present. When doing these or similar activities, we can feel that peace, a halting of our thoughts, if only for a moment. Stop the mind and become present. This is the point where we no longer use the mind to think but allow consciousness to take over. Practice doing this in all day-to-day activities, and it will become habit. The benefits are more peace and less stress.

Bring this practice with you everywhere you go. When you are in the car and the traffic is backed up, just take a deep breath; actually feel the air going into and out of your lungs. It's almost as if you can feel the tension and stress release itself with each exhalation. I usually like to stop my thoughts at night while I lie in bed, trying to go to sleep. Sometimes my mind begins to wander off in so many directions that I can't sleep, which I'm sure happens to most people from time to time. I lie in a comfortable position. Sometimes I close my eyes. Other times, I keep them open and just look into the darkness; pick a spot on the wall, or focus on the ceiling fan as it rotates. Focus and clear your mind of thoughts.

Don't bring your problems into bed with you. I have never heard of anyone solving a problem by tossing and turning, stressing instead of sleeping. Tell yourself that when you get into bed, your problems will just have to wait until morning. And make no exceptions!

## Present Moment

Everyone has experienced the present moment at some point or another. But most people have never understood what is actually taking place. When you experience it, you will begin to crave this inner stillness. Your eyes will open to a brand-new world. Nothing looks the same, smells the same, or feels the same again. It is the telescope concept I mentioned before; instead of looking through the wrong end, we turn it around and are able to see things as we have never seen them before. There is an awakening of the soul.

One thing that has helped me to remember to become still is to set up little reminders. Every time I look at a clock, for example, I notice the time. I remind myself that I am present and everything happening at this particular point in time is in divine order, no matter how I feel about it. I am exactly where I am supposed to be in life.

Regardless of the circumstances of our lives to this point, it is always possible to begin anew. The events of one second ago or fifty years ago are exactly the same—a past moment. Certainly the events can, and often do, have ramifications in our present life situations. I am not saying we can easily forget certain things, or even that we should. What I am saying is that we always have a choice to change this moment. The past can never be undone, the future can never be certain, but this moment is ours.

Painful things or traumatic events are not just going to dissolve once we become present, but a clear-cut path to moving forward will emerge. Maybe you've been fired from a job, are going through a bitter divorce, or lost a loved one. There is no magical cure for the emotional struggles you may face. I can't tell you that if you just do "this" or "that" all your pain will go away. But being locked into the mind, harboring resentment or feeling miserable about anything will only prolong the discomfort.

Questioning the events of the world after the fact, or looking for answers outside of ourselves, is going to lead us on a path that is only beneficial to the survival of the ego. "How can I find work in this economy?" "I can never get close to anyone again, because I can't trust anyone." "I will have a couple drinks or take a few pills, because that will help me forget the pain I feel." These are all the voice of the ego, and they are maniacal and self-destructive. We can never find the answer to anything by looking outside ourselves. Only by embracing the moment can we begin to see. Only by accepting now as the only time there is allows God to communicate through us. Being in this moment lets us make decisions that can help move our lives in the direction we desire.

Acceptance of life is all we really need to give ourselves the fullest life experience. But the world needs to change if we expect to have a place for our children and our children's children. We need to realize our greatness as a species and understand our divinity. And in order for this to take place, we have to be the change.

# 12

## *Be the Change*

In its current state, the world is a dismal place in the eyes of most. Headlines are full of violent acts and hate, the global economy is in the gutter, and millions of people are dying from starvation. Crime is rampant, and wars are killing people by the thousands almost every day. Diseases are spreading, and cancer is claiming lives in unimaginable numbers. The question, for as long as I can remember, is how do we create world peace? How do we stop the madness? What do we have to do to change things?

Most people believe it is beyond our individual control, but the answer to these questions is change can only begin inside ourselves. Each individual must take control over his or her life in order for the change to be realized. It is human nature to point the finger at others and judge others based on our beliefs about how things should be in the world. But the only true way to change our global issues is to look in the mirror and find out what each of us can do to make our own life better.

Once we have realized our true self, our divinity, a lead by example mentality must be established. Our beliefs in the way things are can only be limited by our individual way of living. It is simply a judgment to believe things should be different from the way they are. It's much easier to see someone doing something wrong and then judge the individual for his or her actions. Meanwhile we are doing something another person may condemn. I saw a sign the other day that said something to the effect of, "Don't judge others just because they sin differently than you do."

We have our own ways of looking at the world. We have been raised to see things in a certain way. Looking at others with condemnation over the way they behave will only lead to further division. As it is written in the Bible, Luke 6:41, "Why do you notice the splinter in your brothers' eye but do not see the wooden beam in your own eye?"

Change must begin on an individual level, or as Mahatma Gandhi said, and the quote I opened this book with, "If you want to see change in the world you have to be the change." These words hold one of the greatest lessons we can possess in going forward as a species and in the evolvement of our consciousness. Relying on anyone else to make change happen is only passing the buck or taking the easy way out. It is simply not possible to expect anyone else to be the way we want him or her to be. We must be the example for others. But we cannot show people the way when we have never been that way ourselves. Our actions must bring about a world in which we are happy within ourselves first. Then we will be able to bring that joy out into the world.

It will not always be easy. The temptations of the world and the grasp the ego has on each of us will keep us all slaves until we learn to transcend the mind. We can, however, turn this life into a spiritual practice. From there, we can understand our truest self. It is not enough to simply sit alone and wait for change. "Not alone in the silence but in the busy throng must we all find the way of life," is how Ernest Holmes, in *Creative Mind* (Wilder Publications 2010), explained it.

We cannot sit in the lotus position, meditating for fifteen minutes a day, only to go outside and use the same self-destructive mind-set we had before we sat down. The awakening we must experience is not going to come to most of us in the few minutes each day we devote to meditation or any other spiritual-seeking practices—unless we make it a lifestyle. We all live busy lives. Not many people have the years, months, weeks, or days to commit to sitting under a tree and meditating like the Buddha, or wandering the desert for forty days like Jesus. We must continue living our lives and bring about our awakened consciousness amid the busy throng and among all the seeming madness around us.

When we begin to look at life as the path we are on, where all the obstacles we encounter are actually strategically placed for us to learn the lessons they offer, we can turn all these obstacles into a spiritual practice. To do this, however, we must begin by incorporating the changes we want to see in everyday situations. There will always be a time during the day when you can look at a situation in a different light and see the perfection that placed you under those particular circumstances. Being the change we want to see can become natural to us with enough practice. We don't have to seclude ourselves from the world or leave all our possessions behind to attain this level of living. We don't have to give up anything, unless, of course, it compromises the person we want to be. If this is the case, give it up, and don't look back.

This revolution in change is comprised of only a small group of people now. Learning to become present, questioning the things we don't understand, wanting to see change, and feeling our connection to each other are only the beginning. From here, our numbers will grow. All we have to do is look at all living beings as the perfect creations of a perfect God, and we will understand. Once we remove the blinders, which nearly everyone unknowingly has, we will begin to view the world in a whole different light, one of peace and happiness. We must stop finding fault in a universe that is as perfect as the One who created it.

Finding fault in the world and judging others are counterproductive. We can no longer look at others and see separation. We must realize we are all one and are all divine!

The ego, however, will not go out without a fight. The seemingly tumultuous world, as we witness on our news channels, is a sign the ego is frustrated that peace and happiness are being sought more often than the greed and lust for power of the past. Living in the moment, connecting to Infinity, and changing the world we know are threats to the ego. Without the drama of our life situation, the ego no longer has control. It is death for the ego when it can no longer be the controlling factor in our life. But if we allow the ego to maintain control, it will do whatever it can to be noticed.

Our evolved consciousness will attract others with a similar state of being. But the people with the most ego-driven lives will unite, as well. Like begets like, and an ego can recognize another ego just as easily as positive energy recognizes itself in others. Have you ever noticed that when you are in a bad mood, you often attract confrontations from others with opinions different from yours? How about standing in line at the grocery store and mumbling under your breath about the slowness of the person ahead, and the other person hears you and snaps back? That is your ego attracting the ego of another. The energy level was matched, and like opposite ends of a magnet, they merged. Or, likewise, when you are in a very happy, positive mood, you keep running into people who smile back at you. They seem to be sharing the same type of energy.

This is how our energy flows. The negative energy of the mind attracts other negative energy, while positive, infinite energy attracts the same positivity in others. This is how we will evolve our consciousness on a global scale. The positive energy we bring with us in our awakened state will radiate around the world and even around the entire universe.

It is up to each of us, individually, to ensure we are sending out positive instead of the negative energy into Infinity. We must realize the goodness, which is the perfection of our divinity. As Eckhart Tolle, in *A New Earth: Awakening to Your Life's Purpose* explains, "We do not become good by trying to be good, but by finding the goodness that is already within us, and allowing that goodness to emerge. But it can only emerge if something fundamental changes in your state of consciousness." It is not enough to simply change the way we think in certain situations. We have to change our

# About the Author

C urtis A Vigness grew up in a large family in the rural Midwest but now lives in south Florida. His spiritual experiences have come from his personal quest to know and understand the truth about life. He is passionate about bringing awareness of our spiritual existence to anyone interested in understanding it.